LOGIC PRO & ABLETON LIVE

A STUDENT'S GUIDE TO DAW WORKFLOW AND TECHNIQUES

ARITRA SARKAR

To Di'vai...

Contents

Contents

Foreword

Music production is both an art and a science, requiring a delicate balance between creativity and technical precision. As digital audio workstations (DAWs) continue to revolutionise the industry, aspiring producers, sound engineers, and musicians must equip themselves with a deep understanding of recording, editing, and mixing techniques. This book serves as a comprehensive guide to navigating two of the most powerful DAWs in the music industry—Logic Pro and Ableton Live—providing both foundational knowledge and advanced techniques essential for professional music production.

Whether you are an aspiring producer taking your first steps into the world of digital music or an experienced sound designer seeking to refine your workflow, this book is designed to support your journey. Through structured explanations, step-by-step tutorials, and practical insights, it covers the essential aspects of sound recording, MIDI sequencing, signal processing, audio effects, and mixing strategies. By focusing on industry-standard tools, it ensures that learners develop a strong technical foundation while also nurturing their creative instincts.

One of the greatest advantages of modern music production is accessibility. In the past, professional recordings required expensive studio setups, but today, anyone with a laptop and a DAW can create high-quality music. However, with great accessibility comes the challenge of mastering complex software and workflows. This book simplifies that learning curve by breaking down intricate concepts into clear, actionable steps, allowing students to develop a solid grasp of key production techniques.

As someone who has witnessed the evolution of music production—from analog tape machines to digital workstations—I understand the importance of bridging theory with hands-on practice. This book does just that, making it an indispensable resource for students, educators, and self-taught musicians alike. Each chapter builds upon the previous one, ensuring a structured and progressive learning experience. By the end of this book, you will not only be proficient in Logic Pro and Ableton Live but will also have the confidence to experiment, innovate, and craft your own unique sound.

I invite you to approach this book with curiosity and an eagerness to explore. The world of music production is ever-evolving, and the knowledge contained in these pages will serve as your compass—guiding you through the vast possibilities of digital sound creation.

Aritra Sarkar.

Preface

Music production is an intricate craft that blends technical proficiency with creative expression. With the rise of digital audio workstations (DAWs) such as Logic Pro and Ableton Live, the field has become more accessible than ever. However, mastering these tools requires a deep understanding of their functionality, workflows, and creative applications. This book is designed as a comprehensive question-answer guide, serving as an essential resource for students, aspiring producers, and educators looking to build a strong foundation in music production.

Unlike traditional textbooks that take a theoretical approach, this guide focuses on practical problem-solving, structured in a straightforward question-and-answer format. The aim is to provide quick and direct solutions to common queries that arise while working in Logic Pro and Ableton Live. Whether it is configuring DAW settings, understanding key commands, troubleshooting errors, or learning advanced production techniques, this book presents information in a way that is easy to navigate and apply immediately.

Through structured questions covering core concepts such as audio recording, editing, mixing, MIDI sequencing, effects processing, and workflow optimization, students can develop both technical expertise and creative confidence. By addressing real-world challenges, this book ensures that learners not only understand the theoretical aspects of digital music production but can also implement best practices efficiently.

This book is particularly useful for:

1. Music students who need a structured, accessible reference for learning Logic Pro and Ableton Live.
2. Self-taught producers looking for a reliable troubleshooting guide and quick solutions.
3. Educators and instructors who require a question-based teaching tool for their music production courses.
4. Professional musicians and sound engineers seeking quick tips and workflow enhancements.

With the rapid evolution of music technology, having a concise, reliable, and practical guide to Logic Pro and Ableton Live is invaluable. Whether you are a beginner or an advanced user, this book will help you refine your skills, solve technical issues, and elevate your music production abilities.

I hope that this guide will become your go-to companion in your journey towards mastering digital music production.

Aritra Sarkar

Acknowledgements

The creation of this book has been a deeply rewarding journey, made possible by the collective efforts of many individuals who have contributed their knowledge, insights, and encouragement along the way.

First and foremost, I would like to express my gratitude to the educators, mentors, and industry professionals who have shaped my understanding of music production. Their expertise in Logic Pro, Ableton Live, and digital audio workstations (DAWs) has been instrumental in curating the content of this book in a way that is both practical and accessible for learners at all levels.

I am also deeply appreciative of the music production community—a space where knowledge is shared freely, and creativity thrives. From online forums and discussion groups to experienced professionals willing to share their workflows and techniques, the collective wisdom of this community has greatly influenced the content of this book.

To my colleagues, friends, and family, who have offered their unwavering support and patience during the writing process, I extend my heartfelt gratitude. Their encouragement and belief in this project have been invaluable in bringing this book to life.

This book is dedicated to all those who are passionate about learning, exploring, and mastering the art of music production. I hope that this guide serves as a reliable companion in your journey, helping you navigate the complexities of DAWs with confidence and creativity.

Aritra Sarkar

Prologue

Music production has undergone a radical transformation over the past few decades. What was once confined to large recording studios with expensive analog equipment is now accessible to anyone with a laptop and a digital audio workstation (DAW). With the advent of powerful software such as Logic Pro and Ableton Live, artists and producers can record, edit, and mix professional-grade music from virtually anywhere. However, mastering these tools requires more than just familiarity with the interface—it demands a structured learning approach that combines technical knowledge, practical application, and creative exploration.

This book has been designed as a question-and-answer guide to provide clarity, precision, and ease of learning for students, self-taught producers, and music educators. Unlike traditional textbooks that present linear, theoretical concepts, this book takes a problem-solving approach, directly addressing common challenges and queries that arise when working with Logic Pro and Ableton Live. By structuring the content in a concise and navigable format, this book serves as a quick reference guide for both beginners and advanced users.

Through this comprehensive collection of questions and answers, readers will gain insight into:

1. The fundamentals of DAWs, including digital vs. analog workflows, key commands, and audio settings.
2. Essential recording techniques, from signal flow and gain staging to sample rates and bit-depth settings.
3. Editing and mixing strategies, including automation, audio effects, panning, and mastering concepts.
4. Custom workflows for optimizing efficiency and maximizing creativity in music production.

Beyond the technical aspects, this book aims to empower learners with confidence—allowing them to experiment, troubleshoot, and push the boundaries of their creative potential. The goal is not just to teach but to equip producers with the necessary skills to navigate their DAW seamlessly, making informed creative decisions along the way.

Whether you are a music student, an aspiring sound engineer, a DJ, or a professional artist, this book is intended to be your go-to companion for mastering Logic Pro and Ableton Live. With clear, concise, and practical solutions, it ensures that every reader can unlock their full potential in music production.

Welcome to a journey where sound meets innovation, knowledge fuels creativity, and music production becomes an intuitive, seamless process.

Aritra Sarkar

ONE

ESSENTIAL COMMANDS, SHORTCUTS, AND KEY CONCEPTS

Logic Pro Key Commands and Concepts

General Navigation

- Play/Stop: Spacebar
- Return to the beginning: Return key
- Cycle mode on/off: C
- Zoom in/out horizontally: Command + Left/Right Arrow
- Zoom vertically: Command + Up/Down Arrow

Editing Tools

- Pointer Tool: Press T, then T again
- Pencil Tool: T, then P
- Scissors Tool: T, then I
- Fade Tool: T, then A
- Marquee Tool: T, then R

Recording and MIDI

- Record: R
- Punch recording: Control + Option + Command + P
- Quantize MIDI notes: Q (in Piano Roll)
- MIDI Velocity Adjust: Command + Drag on notes

Automation

- Show/hide automation: A
- Add automation point: Control + Click on automation line
- Delete automation point: Option + Click
- Snap automation: Shift + Click while dragging

Mixer and Channel Controls

- Mute/Unmute track: M
- Solo track: S

Adjust volume: Drag the fader in the mixer (Command + Drag for fine-tuning)

Ableton Live Key Commands and Concepts

General Navigation

- Play/Stop: Spacebar
- Return to Start: Shift + Spacebar
- Switch between Session/Arrangement View: Tab
- Zoom in/out: Command + = / Command + –

Editing and Clips

- Duplicate Clip: Command + D
- Loop selection: Command + L
- Consolidate clips: Command + J
- Split Clip: Command + E

MIDI and Recording

- Arm track for recording: Command + Shift + M
- Quantize MIDI notes: Command + U
- MIDI Capture (after playing without recording): Shift + Command + C

Automation and Effects

- Show/hide automation: A
- Add automation point: Command + Click
- Delete automation point: Option + Click
- Adjust automation curve: Shift + Drag

Mixer Controls

- Mute track: 0 (zero)
- Solo track: S
- Volume adjust: Drag fader or Command + Drag for fine-tuning

Step-by-step explanation of the key concepts

1. Grid Adjustment (Logic Pro & Ableton Live)

- Purpose: Ensures precise alignment of audio and MIDI regions to the musical grid.

  In Logic Pro:

- Increase Grid Size: Press Command + 1 to increase grid resolution (fewer subdivisions).
- Decrease Grid Size: Press Command + 2 to decrease grid resolution (more subdivisions).
- Smart Grid: Automatically adjusts grid resolution based on zoom level. Enable it in the Snap menu by selecting Smart.
- Custom Grid: Use the Snap settings menu in the toolbar to select divisions like Bar, Beat, Division, or Tick for detailed editing.

  In Ableton Live:

- Toggle Grid Settings: Right-click in the Arrangement or Clip View to select Fixed Grid or Adaptive Grid.

  Shortcuts:

- Command + 1 – Increase grid size.
- Command + 2 – Decrease grid size.
- Command + 4 – Toggle grid snapping on/off.
- Advanced Tip: Use Triplet Grids (Shift + Command + 3) for complex rhythms and polyrhythms.

  2. Flex Time (Logic Pro)

- Purpose: Adjust timing of audio without slicing it.

  Steps to Use:

- Select an audio track and enable Flex mode by clicking the Flex button (Command + F).
- Choose a Flex algorithm depending on the audio type:

  - Rhythmic for drums.
  - Monophonic for single-note melodies.
  - Polyphonic for chords.

- Adjust timing by dragging Flex markers on the waveform.
- Use Quantize in the Region Inspector to snap all audio to the grid.
- Advanced Tip: Adjust the Flex Smoothing parameter for natural sound.

3. Warping (Ableton Live)

- Purpose: Time-stretch audio for perfect sync with your project.

Steps to Use:

- Double-click on an audio clip to open the Clip View.
- Enable Warp if it's not already active.
- Add Warp Markers by double-clicking on the transient markers.
- Drag Warp Markers to align beats with the grid.
- Choose the Warp mode suitable for your audio:

  - Beats for drums.
  - Tones for monophonic melodies.
  - Complex Pro for full tracks.

Shortcuts:

- Shift + Click – Add Warp Marker.
- Delete – Remove Warp Marker.

Advanced Tip: Use Grain Size and Flux in the Warp settings for unique granular effects.

4. MIDI Mapping (Logic Pro & Ableton Live)

- Purpose: Assign hardware knobs, faders, and buttons to control software parameters.

In Logic Pro:

- Open Controller Assignments (Command + K).
- Move the hardware control you want to map.
- Click on the Logic parameter you wish to control.
- Press Learn to assign the control.
- Advanced Tip: Use Zones and Modes in Controller Assignments for layered control sets.

In Ableton Live:

- Press Command + M to enter MIDI mapping mode.
- Click on the software parameter you want to control.
- Move the hardware control to assign it.
- Exit MIDI mapping mode by pressing Command + M again.
- Advanced Tip: Use the Min/Max range in the mapping browser to limit control ranges.

5. Automation (Logic Pro & Ableton Live)

- Purpose: Automate changes in parameters like volume, panning, effects, etc.

In Logic Pro:

- Press A to reveal automation lanes.
- Choose the parameter from the Automation Parameter dropdown.
- Draw automation points using the Pointer Tool (Command + Click).
- Adjust curves by clicking and dragging between points.
- Advanced Tip: Use Relative Automation to add adjustments without overwriting existing automation.

In Ableton Live:

- Press A to reveal the automation lanes.

- Click on a parameter and draw automation curves directly in the clip or arrangement.
- Shortcut: Shift + Click to create multiple automation breakpoints.
- Advanced Tip: Use Clip Automation for per-clip modulation independent of the track automation.

6. Quantization (Logic Pro & Ableton Live)

- Purpose: Align MIDI notes to the grid for precise timing.

In Logic Pro:

- Select MIDI notes and press Q to quantize.
- Adjust the Quantize Strength slider for subtle corrections.
- Use Swing values for humanized grooves.

In Ableton Live:

- Select MIDI notes and press Command + U to quantize.
- Use Shift + Command + U to open the quantize settings.
- Adjust the Amount slider for varying quantization strengths.

Advanced Tip: Quantize audio clips with Warp enabled for timing correction.

7. Sampling and Samplers (Logic Pro & Ableton Live)
In Logic Pro (Quick Sampler):

- Drag an audio file into Quick Sampler.
- Use Slice Mode to auto-slice samples by transients.
- Map slices to MIDI keys.
- Adjust ADSR envelopes for dynamic control.

In Ableton Live (Simpler & Sampler):

- Drag audio into Simpler.
- Choose Slice Mode and click Slice to MIDI.
- Adjust the Warp Mode for seamless looping.

- Use Sampler for advanced modulations, like multi-zone key mapping and filter envelopes.

8. Track Stacks (Logic Pro)

- Purpose: Combine multiple tracks into one group for processing.

Steps to Use:

- Select multiple tracks.
- Right-click and choose Create Track Stack.
- Select Folder Stack for simple grouping or Summing Stack for shared processing.
- Add effects on the stack track for global processing.

9. Racks (Ableton Live)

- Purpose: Group instruments and effects for complex setups.

Steps to Use:

- Select multiple devices (instruments or effects).
- Press Command + G to group them into a rack.
- Add Macros by clicking Map and assigning parameters to macro knobs.
- Use Chain Selector for layered sound design.

Additional Key Concepts for Mastery:

- Key Commands (Memorize essential shortcuts for speed).
- Clip Envelopes (Ableton): Automate parameters within individual clips.
- Smart Tempo (Logic): Match the project tempo to audio recordings.
- Freeze Tracks: Temporarily render tracks to save CPU.
- Sidechain Compression: Duck audio dynamically based on another track's signal.
- Groove Templates: Extract rhythm from one clip and apply it to another.
- Multiband Compression: Control different frequency ranges independently.

Recording Audio into the Quick Sampler

- Open Quick Sampler: Insert Quick Sampler on a software instrument track.
- Select 'Record' Mode: Click the 'Record' button in the Quick Sampler interface.
- Choose Input Source: Use the dropdown to select your audio input device.
- Arm Track and Record: Enable recording, then click the record button to capture audio directly into the sampler.

Tip: Ensure your input level is set correctly to avoid clipping.
Start and End Markers in Logic

- Purpose: Define playback regions within an audio file.
- Usage:

  - Drag the markers to set the start and end points.
  - Useful for trimming and looping without affecting the original audio.

- Pro Tip: Use precise markers for seamless loops and cleaner edits.

Loop Start and End Markers

- Function: Specify the looped section of an audio sample.
- Steps:

  - Place the markers at desired points.
  - Adjust dynamically for perfect loop transitions.

- Use Case: Ideal for creating pads or repetitive rhythmic patterns.

Crossfade Marker

- Purpose: Ensures smooth audio transitions within loops.
- Method:

- ◦ Drag the crossfade handle between loop points.
- ◦ Adjust crossfade length for blending.

- Benefit: Eliminates audio glitches during loop playback.

Fade In and Fade Out Markers

- Function: Gradually increase or decrease volume.
- Steps:

- ◦ Drag the fade handles at the start or end.
- ◦ Set fade duration for subtle or rapid transitions.

- Tip: Essential for preventing sudden audio cuts.

Slice Markers in Logic Pro

- Purpose: Splits an audio sample into slices.
- How-To:

- ◦ Enable 'Slice' mode in Quick Sampler.
- ◦ Adjust slice points manually or automatically.

- Use Case: Perfect for drum loops and chopped vocals.

Flex Mode in Quick Sampler

- Enables: Time-stretching and pitch-shifting independently.
- Steps:

- ◦ Click the 'Flex' button.
- ◦ Choose an algorithm (e.g., rhythmic, monophonic).

- Benefit: Maintain audio quality while adjusting tempo or pitch.

Manipulating ADSR in Quick Sampler

- Controls:

- ○ Attack: Time to reach peak volume.
- ○ Decay: Time to settle at sustain level.
- ○ Sustain: Volume during hold.
- ○ Release: Fade-out time.

- Pro Tip: Use short attack for percussive sounds and long release for ambient pads.

Adding a Pitch Envelope

- Steps:

  - ○ Go to 'Modulation' > 'Pitch'.
  - ○ Adjust ADSR for pitch modulation.
  - ○ Set range and amount.

- Use Case: Adds pitch bends and dynamic sound variations.

Snap Modes in Quick Sampler

- Types:

  - ○ Off: Free movement.
  - ○ Smart: Context-based snapping.
  - ○ Bar/Beat/Division/Tick: Snaps to grid units.

- Tip: Use 'Smart' for quick edits and 'Bar' for precise rhythmic samples.

Loop Modes in Quick Sampler

- Types:

  - ○ No Loop: Single playback.
  - ○ Forward Loop: Repeats forward.
  - ○ Reverse Loop: Loops backward.
  - ○ Ping-Pong Loop: Alternates directions.

- Pro Tip: Use Ping-Pong for evolving textures.

Glide Between Notes

- Steps:

  - Go to 'Pitch' > 'Glide'.
  - Adjust time for smooth transitions.

- Use Case: Ideal for expressive leads and basslines.

Additional Key Concepts for Quick Sampler:

- Normalization: Balances audio levels within the sampler.
- Root Key Detection: Sets the pitch reference for samples.
- Velocity Sensitivity: Adjusts sample response to MIDI velocity.
- One-Shot Mode: Plays the entire sample regardless of key hold duration.
- Multi-Sampling: Load multiple samples for different pitch ranges.

TWO

INTRODUCTION TO LOGIC

1. Explain briefly with an example, how recordings were done using analog equipment in the past.

- Analog recordings were created using magnetic tape recorders. Sound from instruments or microphones was captured as an electrical signal, which was then magnetically imprinted onto tape. For example, in the 1960s, The Beatles recorded using a Studer J37 four-track tape machine at Abbey Road Studios. Editing required cutting and splicing the tape physically, and effects like reverb were achieved using mechanical means, such as echo chambers.

2. Make a comparison between digital and analog recordings.

- Analog: Uses continuous signals stored on tape or vinyl. It often has a "warm" sound due to natural harmonic distortions but is prone to noise and degradation over time.
- Digital: Converts sound into binary code, offering precise editing and high fidelity. Digital recordings are more versatile, easily stored, and shared, though they may be criticised for being too "sterile" compared to analog warmth.

3. What do you understand by the term DAW?

- A Digital Audio Workstation (DAW) is software used for recording, editing, mixing, and producing audio. Examples include Logic Pro, Ableton Live, and Pro Tools. DAWs provide virtual tools such as synthesizers, samplers, and effects, replacing traditional studio equipment.

4. How do you reset Logic?

- To reset Logic Pro, you can delete its preferences:

  - Close Logic Pro.
  - Go to ~/Library/Preferences.
  - Delete the file com.apple.logic10.plist.
  - Reopen Logic Pro, and it will create a new preference file with default settings.

5. How do you activate the advanced tools in Logic?

- Go to Logic Pro > Preferences > Advanced Tools.
- Tick the box for Show Advanced Tools.
- You can enable individual advanced features such as audio editing, surround sound, and MIDI programming from this menu.

6. Demonstrate how you would search for a Key command in Logic.

- Open Logic Pro and go to Logic Pro > Key Commands > Edit.
- In the search bar at the top, type the name or function you are looking for.
- Results will display all relevant key commands, which can be viewed or modified.

7. Can you make your own key commands in Logic? If yes, then demonstrate.

- Yes:

  - Go to Logic Pro > Key Commands > Edit.
  - Find the command you want to assign a shortcut to.

- ◦ Click Learn by Key Label, then press the key combination you wish to use.
- ◦ Click Assign to save the custom key command.

8. How can you reset key commands in Logic?

- Open Logic Pro > Key Commands > Edit.
- Click Options > Initialize All Key Commands to restore the default settings.

9. How can you export/import key commands in Logic? Are there any benefits to this practice?

- To export, go to Logic Pro > Key Commands > Edit > Options > Export Key Commands and save the file.
- To import, choose Import Key Commands from the same menu.
- Benefits: Exporting allows you to back up your customised shortcuts, share them across different devices, or revert easily to a known configuration after changes.

10. Describe the contents of the Control Bar, Track Area and Inspector in Logic respectively.

- Control Bar: Located at the top, it contains buttons for transport controls (play, record, stop), cycle, tempo, and metronome settings.
- Track Area: The main workspace where audio, MIDI, and automation tracks are arranged in a timeline.
- Inspector: On the left side, it provides detailed information and controls for the selected track, including volume, pan, effects, and MIDI settings.

11. What is the key command for saving a project in Logic?

- The key command for saving a project in Logic Pro is Command (⌘) + S.

12. How can you copy regions using keyboard shortcuts?

- Select the region you want to copy.
- Press Command (⌘) + C to copy.

- Move the playhead to the desired location and press Command (⌘) + V to paste.
- Alternatively, hold Option (⌥) while dragging the region to create a copy.

13. How can you loop a particular region?

- Select the region.
- Press L on your keyboard, and the region will loop continuously based on its length.

14. Define Audio Tracks and Software Instrument Tracks.

- Audio Tracks: Used to record and playback audio files such as vocals, guitar recordings, or imported audio samples.
- Software Instrument Tracks: Used to create and play virtual instruments using MIDI data, such as synthesizers, pianos, or drum machines within Logic Pro.

15. How can you add new tracks to Logic?

- Click the + button above the track headers or press Option (⌥) + Command (⌘) + N.
- Choose either Audio Track, Software Instrument Track, or Drummer Track in the pop-up window and click Create.

16. What is an Apple Loop?

- An Apple Loop is a pre-recorded musical phrase or rhythm that can be looped seamlessly and automatically matches the tempo and key of your project in Logic Pro.

17. What is the format of an Apple Loop?

- Apple Loops are in CAF (Core Audio Format) or AIFF format, which stores both audio and metadata for tempo, key, and time signature.

18. How do you search for Apple Loops in the Loop folder under categories of Instruments and Genre?

- Open the Loop Browser by clicking the loop icon or pressing O.
- Use the filter columns to search by Instrument, Genre, or Mood, and type keywords into the search bar to refine your results.

19. How do you copy tracks in Logic?

- Right-click the track header and select Duplicate Track or press Command (⌘) + D to create an identical copy of the track with all settings intact.

20. How do you choose and mark favourites among Apple Loops in the Loop folder?

- In the Loop Browser, right-click on a loop and select Add to Favorites.
- You can view your favourites by selecting the Favorites category in the Loop Browser.

21. How do you cycle in Logic?

- Cycling in Logic Pro allows you to repeatedly play a selected portion of your project.

  - To enable Cycle mode, press C on your keyboard or click the Cycle button (two arrows forming a circle) in the Control Bar.
  - Drag the yellow Cycle region in the ruler area above your tracks to define the section you want to loop.
  - You can adjust the start and end points by dragging the edges of the Cycle region, and Logic will continuously loop playback within this selection, useful for editing and fine-tuning.

22. Explain how we could change the information being displayed in the LCD display according to our preferences.

- The LCD display in Logic Pro provides critical project information such as tempo, time signature, and playback position. To customise it:

  - Right-click the LCD display and choose between different modes such as Beats & Time, Custom, or Large Display.

- ◦ In Custom mode, you can right-click and select which parameters to show, such as CPU load, sample rate, and timecode, tailoring the display to your needs for enhanced workflow efficiency.

23. What is the function of Catch Playhead?

- The Catch Playhead feature ensures that the playhead remains visible during playback or recording.

  - ◦ Activated by clicking the Catch button (a small icon with a playhead and a dot) or pressing Shift + Command + C, it automatically scrolls the workspace to keep up with the playhead's movement, particularly useful for long projects.

24. How does Logic's LCD display present information by default?

- By default, Logic's LCD display shows:

  - ◦ Playhead Position: Displayed in bars, beats, divisions, and ticks.
  - ◦ Tempo: The current tempo in beats per minute (BPM).
  - ◦ Time Signature: Indicates the meter, e.g., 4/4 or 3/4.
  - ◦ Cycle Area: Shows if cycling is enabled and the loop range.
  - ◦ Project Length: Displays the total duration of the project.

- This default setup provides essential information for tracking project progress, timing, and structure.

25. How can you set the key signature and tempo for any project in Logic?

- Open the Inspector by pressing I.
- In the Project Settings, select the Key Signature dropdown to choose your key.
- To set the tempo, either adjust the Tempo field in the LCD display manually or use the Tempo Track (press Global Tracks button and enable Tempo Track) to create tempo changes over time.

26. How can you add Audio FX to any track in Logic?

- Open the Mixer (press X) or use the Inspector.
- Click on an empty Audio FX slot on a track.
- Choose from Logic's built-in effects (such as EQ, reverb, or compression) or load third-party plugins.
- You can also chain multiple effects, adjust their parameters, and automate them for creative sound design or precise mixing.

27. How can you pan individual tracks in Logic?

- Panning controls the left-right stereo positioning of audio.

  - In the Track Header or Mixer, locate the Pan knob.
  - Drag it left or right to position the audio in the stereo field.
  - For more advanced panning, use Stereo Pan by right-clicking the pan knob, allowing you to control the spread and direction of stereo tracks, crucial for achieving a balanced mix.

28. How do you turn off Normalize while exporting audio from Logic?

- Normalization adjusts audio levels to a standard peak, but it's often avoided for professional mixing.

  - Go to File > Bounce > Project or Section.
  - In the Bounce window, uncheck Normalize under the Audio options before exporting to preserve your original mix levels.

29. How do you stop clipping if it happens in Logic?

- Clipping occurs when audio levels exceed the maximum limit, causing distortion.

  - Lower the track's volume fader in the Mixer.
  - Use Gain plugins to adjust levels pre-fader.
  - Apply a Limiter to ensure peaks don't exceed the ceiling.
  - Check the Master Output meter and maintain levels below 0 dBFS to avoid digital clipping.

30. How do you export audio in MP3 from Logic? How do you export audio in WAV in Ableton?

- In Logic Pro, go to File > Bounce > Project or Section.
- Choose MP3 in the bounce settings and adjust the bit rate as needed.
- In Ableton Live, go to File > Export Audio/Video.
- Select WAV as the file type, adjust sample rate and bit depth, and export your file.

31. How do you play Apple Loops in the key of the project you are working on? How do you play apples in their original recorded key in Logic?

- To play Apple Loops in the key of your project:

  - Open the Loop Browser by pressing O.
  - Drag the desired loop into your project. Logic Pro automatically matches the loop's key to your project's key, provided that the Follow Tempo and Key checkbox in the Loop Browser is enabled.

- To play loops in their original recorded key:

  - After dragging the loop into your project, select the region.
  - In the Region Inspector, uncheck Follow Tempo & Pitch.
  - This disables Logic's automatic pitch adjustment, allowing the loop to play in its original key.

- This flexibility helps producers maintain harmonic consistency across a project or preserve the authentic pitch of recorded samples when needed.

32. How do you search for all Apple Loops that are in a Major key?

- Open the Loop Browser by pressing O or clicking the Loop icon in the Control Bar.
- In the search bar, type Major.
- You can also use the Filter by Key option by clicking the Key menu in the Loop Browser and selecting Major.
- Logic will display all Apple Loops tagged with a Major key signature, allowing you to incorporate harmonically suitable loops into your

project.

33. How do you search for all Apple Loops having the time signature 3/4?

- Open the Loop Browser.
- In the Loop Browser filter columns, click on the Time Signature column.
- Select 3/4 from the dropdown list.
- Alternatively, you can type 3/4 in the search bar, and Logic will filter loops that have the 3/4 time signature, essential for waltz rhythms or compound time compositions.

34. Where are the transport controls located in Logic?

- The Transport Controls are located at the top of the Logic Pro interface in the Control Bar. This section includes essential playback and recording controls such as:

  - Play, Stop, Record, Rewind, Fast Forward, Cycle (Loop), and Metronome buttons.

- These controls allow you to navigate through your project efficiently during editing, recording, and mixing.

35. How do you increase the gain on a region in Logic?

- To increase the gain:

  - Select the audio region.
  - In the Region Inspector on the left, find the Gain slider and drag it to the right to increase the gain.
  - Alternatively, open the Mixer (press X), and adjust the Gain plugin if inserted on the track.

- Increasing gain helps balance levels without affecting the overall track volume.

36. How do you transpose a region in Logic?

- Select the region in the Track Area.
- In the Region Inspector, find the Transpose field.
- Enter a value (e.g., +2 for two semitones up or -3 for three semitones down).
- For finer control, use the MIDI Transform tool for MIDI regions.
- This is essential for pitch correction, harmonization, or creative effects.

37. How do you reverse an audio sample in Logic?

- Select the audio region.
- Open the File Editor (press E).
- In the editor, click Functions > Reverse.
- The waveform flips horizontally, playing the audio backwards, often used for creative sound design like reverse cymbals or atmospheric effects.

38. How do you mute a region in Logic?

- Select the region and press Control + M to mute it.
- Alternatively, right-click the region and choose Mute.
- Muted regions are visually greyed out but remain in place, useful during editing without deleting content.

39. How do you add regions to your Loop Library in Logic?

- Select the region you want to add.
- Right-click and choose Add to Apple Loops Library.
- Name the loop, assign metadata such as genre, key, and time signature, and click Create.
- This custom loop is then accessible in the Loop Browser, streamlining future projects.

40. How can you favourite loops in Logic?

- Open the Loop Browser (press O).
- Right-click any loop and select Add to Favorites.
- You can view all favourited loops by clicking the Favorites category in the Loop Browser, making it easier to access preferred sounds.

41. Where is the inspector and what are its uses?

- The Inspector is located on the left side of the Logic Pro window (press I to show/hide).
- It displays essential controls such as:

    ◦ Track Parameters (Volume, Pan, Effects)
    ◦ Region Parameters (Gain, Transpose, Quantize)
    ◦ Channel Strip settings

- It serves as a central hub for track and region modifications without needing to open the Mixer or individual plugins.

42. Where is the tracks area and what does it contain?

- The Tracks Area is the main workspace in Logic Pro, occupying most of the interface.
- It contains:

    ◦ Audio Tracks, MIDI Tracks, Automation Lanes, and Regions (Audio/ MIDI).

- This area is where you arrange, edit, and layer your recordings, loops, and instruments.

43. Where is the control bar and what does it contain?

- The Control Bar is at the top of the Logic Pro window.
- It contains:

    ◦ Transport Controls (Play, Record, Stop, Cycle)
    ◦ Tempo, Time Signature, Key Signature displays
    ◦ Tools for Automation, Snap, and Quantize settings

- It offers quick access to key project settings and playback controls, enhancing workflow efficiency.

44. Where is the workspace and what does it contain?

- The Workspace refers to the combined area of the Tracks Area, Mixer, and Editors.
- It contains:

  - All Audio/MIDI regions, Automation lanes, and visual representations of your project's components.

- This is the core area where editing, arranging, and mixing occur, integrating all project elements seamlessly.

45. When multiple panes are open, how do you make sure the pane you want reacts to the key commands?

- When multiple panes (such as the Mixer, Editor, and Tracks Area) are open, Logic Pro allows you to set a specific pane to respond to key commands:

  - Click inside the pane you want to control. A thin blue border will appear around it, indicating it is the active pane.
  - Only the active pane responds to key commands, ensuring that actions like copy, paste, or playback controls affect the intended area.

- This feature prevents unintended edits when working with multiple sections simultaneously.

46. Describe two ways of changing numeric value in Logic.

- There are two primary methods to change numeric values in Logic Pro:

  - Click and Drag Method:

    - Click on the numeric value (e.g., tempo, volume, transpose) and drag your mouse up or down to increase or decrease the value incrementally.

  - Direct Input Method:

- Double-click on the numeric value, type the desired number, and press Enter to apply it.

- Both methods provide flexibility depending on whether you need fine adjustments or precise values.

47. How do you resize a region in Logic?

- To resize an audio or MIDI region in Logic Pro:

  - Move your mouse to the lower-left or lower-right corner of the region. The pointer will change to a trim tool (a bracket with arrows).
  - Click and drag inward to shorten the region or outward to extend it.
  - Alternatively, select the region and adjust the Length field in the Region Inspector for exact resizing.

- This allows precise control over region length, crucial for arranging and editing.

48. In the help tag, what are the units of the four numeric values used to determine the length and position of a region?

- The four numeric values in Logic's help tag are displayed as:

  - Bars | Beats | Divisions | Ticks
  - Bars: Represent full measures of music (e.g., 4/4 time has 4 beats per bar).
  - Beats: Individual beats within a bar.
  - Divisions: Subdivisions of a beat, set by the project's division setting (e.g., 1/16 or 1/32).
  - Ticks: The smallest unit of time in Logic Pro, with 240 ticks per division, used for ultra-fine positioning and timing adjustments.

49. How many ticks are there in a sixteenth note?

- In Logic Pro, a sixteenth note is composed of 240 ticks.

- ○ Since a quarter note contains 960 ticks, and a sixteenth note is one-quarter of a quarter note, the math is: $960 \div 4 = 240$ ticks960 \div 4 = 240 \text{ ticks}960÷4=240 ticks

- This precision is vital for quantizing, editing MIDI, and ensuring tight rhythmic accuracy.

THREE
INTRODUCTION TO ABLETON

1. What are two ways in which we can toggle between Session View and Arrangement View?

- Ableton Live offers two primary ways to switch between the Session View and the Arrangement View, each designed to accommodate different workflows:

  - Using Keyboard Shortcuts:

    - Press Tab on your keyboard to toggle instantly between the Session View and Arrangement View.
    - This shortcut is one of the most commonly used in Ableton because it allows quick and seamless navigation during both live performances and production sessions.

  - Using the View Selector Buttons:

    - At the top-right corner of the Ableton interface, you will find two small icons:

      - The grid icon (Session View) represents the non-linear clip-based view, ideal for live performances and improvisation.
      - The timeline icon (Arrangement View) represents the linear track-based view, suitable for detailed arranging, editing, and

mixing.

- Clicking these icons switches the workspace from one view to the other.

- Bonus Insight for Scoring Higher: The Session View is often used for launching clips, loops, and samples in a free-form manner, while the Arrangement View is used to sequence and arrange entire tracks in a traditional left-to-right timeline. Mastering the ability to switch between these views efficiently is critical in both performance and production workflows in Ableton Live.

Control Bar

1. What is Ableton Link and how do we use it?

- Ableton Link is a technology that allows users to synchronise tempo across multiple devices running Ableton Live or other Link-enabled software, wirelessly over a local network.
- Usage:

  - Enable Link by clicking the Link button in the Control Bar.
  - Once enabled, any other device on the same network with Link activated will sync to the same tempo, making it ideal for collaborative performances, DJ sets, or integrating with mobile apps like Launchpad or Traktor.

2. What does the Tap Tempo button do?

- The Tap Tempo button lets users manually set the project's tempo by clicking the button repeatedly at the desired speed.

  - Located in the Control Bar, tapping it in rhythm adjusts the tempo accordingly, useful for live performances where the tempo needs to be synced manually with external instruments or live bands.

3. What are two ways of altering Tempo Values in Ableton?

- Method 1: Tempo Box in Control Bar – Click the tempo value at the top-left of the Control Bar and type a new BPM or drag up/down with the mouse.
- Method 2: Tempo Automation – In the Arrangement View, create automation lanes for the Master track and adjust the Tempo automation line to change tempo over time.

4. What function does the Tempo Nudge Up and Tempo Nudge Down buttons serve?

- These buttons temporarily speed up or slow down the project's tempo to match an external source, such as syncing with a live band or a DJ track.

  - Nudge Up (arrow up) slightly increases tempo.
  - Nudge Down (arrow down) slightly decreases tempo.

- This is particularly useful for aligning beats on the fly during performances.

5. How do we change Time Signature in Ableton?

- In the Control Bar, next to the tempo display, you'll find the Time Signature field.
- Click on it and enter the desired time signature (e.g., 3/4 or 7/8).
- You can also automate time signature changes in the Arrangement View using the Master track's signature automation lane.

6. What function does Global Quantize serve?

- Global Quantize ensures that any clip, loop, or MIDI note triggered aligns perfectly to the project's grid, preventing timing errors.

  - Located in the Control Bar, it offers options such as 1 Bar, 1/4, 1/8, etc..
  - For instance, with 1 Bar Quantize, triggering a clip waits until the next full bar starts, ensuring tight rhythmic synchronisation during playback.

7. What is the function of the Follow button and what are the two types of follow behaviour?

- The Follow button keeps the Arrangement View scrolling in real-time during playback, ensuring the current playback position remains visible.
- Two types of follow behaviour:

  - Continuous Follow: The screen continuously scrolls as the playhead moves.
  - Page Follow: The screen jumps to the next section when the playhead reaches the end of the visible area, ideal for precise editing and

reviewing sections in longer arrangements.

8. What are Transport Controls in Ableton?

- Transport Controls include the essential playback buttons located in the Control Bar:

  - Play, Stop, Record, Loop (Cycle), and Tap Tempo.

- They allow you to control playback, start/stop recording, and manage looping, much like a traditional tape recorder but in a digital format.

9. How to make custom shortcuts in Ableton and save them for future use?

- Go to Options > Edit Key Map (or press Command + K on Mac).
- Click the function you want to assign a shortcut to, then press the key you wish to use.
- Press Command + K again to exit Key Mapping mode, and your shortcuts will be saved for future sessions.

10. What function does the CPU load meter serve?

- The CPU load meter displays the current CPU usage in real-time, showing how much processing power Ableton Live is consuming.

  - High CPU usage can lead to audio dropouts or lag, so monitoring this helps in optimising performance by managing plugins, samples, and effects.

11. How can we use the CPU load meter as a panic button?

- Clicking the CPU load meter when it spikes can act as a panic button by stopping all currently playing audio, clips, and effects immediately, preventing crashes or glitches during a live performance.

12. How do we check for overloads in Ableton?

- The Overload Indicator next to the CPU load meter lights up red when the CPU load is too high, indicating audio processing overload.
- Users can manage overloads by reducing active tracks, freezing tracks (right-click a track and select Freeze Track), or reducing plugin usage.

13. What function does the Loop Switch serve?

- The Loop Switch (circular arrow icon) in the Control Bar enables or disables looping for the selected region in the Arrangement View.

  ○ When activated, the selected section loops continuously during playback, essential for working on short sections, live looping, or refining a specific part of a project.

Browser

1. How do we show/hide the Browser in Ableton?

- To show or hide the Browser, press Command + Option + B on Mac or Ctrl + Alt + B on Windows.
- Alternatively, click the small triangle icon in the top-left corner of the screen.
- This allows users to toggle the Browser view, essential for managing space when working on complex projects.

2. What is the shortcut for searching the Browser?

- The shortcut for searching within the Browser is Command + F on Mac or Ctrl + F on Windows.
- This instantly activates the search bar, allowing users to quickly locate instruments, effects, samples, or plugins without manually browsing.

3. What purpose does Collections serve in Ableton? How can we add/ remove Browser components into Collections?

- Collections are user-defined categories in the Browser for organizing frequently used items such as sounds, effects, or plugins.
- To add items, right-click on any Browser component and select Add to Collection, then choose a colour-coded collection.
- To remove an item, right-click the component and select Remove from Collection.
- Collections streamline workflow by keeping essential tools easily accessible.

4. What does the Categories section of the Browser contain? Provide a brief explanation for its contents.

- The Categories section includes predefined categories such as:

    ○ Sounds: All instrument sounds like drums, bass, and pads.
    ○ Drums: Drum racks, samples, and percussion kits.

- Instruments: All virtual instruments including Ableton's built-in synthesizers and samplers.
- Audio Effects: Built-in effects like EQs, reverbs, and compressors.
- MIDI Effects: MIDI-specific tools such as arpeggiators and chord generators.
- Samples: All imported and stock audio samples.

- This section provides a comprehensive and organised view of all available content within Ableton Live.

5. How can we insert effects in Ableton's tracks?

- Open the Browser and navigate to Audio Effects or MIDI Effects.
- Drag the desired effect directly onto a track in the Session View or Arrangement View.
- Alternatively, double-click the effect, and it will be added to the selected track's device chain.
- This method ensures quick and intuitive effect placement during sound design and mixing.

6. Where are 3rd party plugins and libraries located in Ableton?

- Third-party plugins are found under the Plug-ins category in the Browser.
- Installed libraries appear under the Places section, typically in the Packs folder or User Library, where custom content and imported libraries are stored.

7. What are the different components of the Places section of the Browser and what function do they serve?

- Places contains user-defined locations for files and folders, including:

  - Packs: Ableton sound packs and libraries.
  - User Library: All user-created content such as presets and samples.
  - Current Project: Files related to the active project.
  - Add Folder: Custom folders added by the user for quick access.

- Each component allows quick navigation and organisation of project files, samples, and custom libraries.

8. Where can we find Ableton's Core Library within the Browser?

- The Core Library is located under Packs in the Browser.
- It contains Ableton's built-in sounds, instruments, drum kits, and effect presets, serving as the foundational content library for music production in Ableton Live.

9. How can we add/remove custom folders into the Browser?

- To add a folder, click Add Folder in the Places section, navigate to the desired folder, and select it.
- To remove a folder, right-click the folder in Places and choose Remove from Sidebar.
- This feature allows users to customise their Browser for quicker access to frequently used files and folders.

10. What function does the Preview button in the Browser serve?

- The Preview button (a small headphone icon) allows users to listen to samples, loops, and audio files directly in the Browser before importing them into the project.
- This ensures that only suitable sounds are added to the project, saving time during sound selection.

11. What function does the Raw button in the Browser serve?

- The Raw button disables time-stretching when previewing audio files, playing them at their original tempo and pitch.
- This is useful when users need to hear the unmodified version of a sample before deciding how it fits into their project.

Miscellaneous

1. What is the Info View? How can we use it as a custom notepad?

- Info View provides brief descriptions of interface elements when hovered over with the mouse.
- To open it, click the question mark icon in the lower-left corner or press Shift + ?.
- As a custom notepad, drag an Empty MIDI Clip into the session and use the Clip Notes section to jot down project details, acting as a built-in notepad.

2. What is the Device View and how can we open/close it quickly?

- Device View displays all instruments, effects, and devices on a selected track.
- Toggle it quickly by pressing Shift + Tab or clicking the small arrow icon in the bottom-right corner.

3. How can you toggle between Device View and Clip View?

- Press Shift + Tab to alternate between Device View and Clip View.
- Clip View displays MIDI notes or audio waveforms for editing, while Device View shows the applied instruments and effects.

4. What is the Time Ruler and Bar Ruler in Ableton and what purpose do they serve?

- Time Ruler: Located at the top, displays time in minutes and seconds.
- Bar Ruler: Shows musical time in bars and beats, essential for rhythmic alignment during editing.

5. How to change Grid Size in Ableton using keyboard shortcuts?

- Press Command + 1 to increase grid resolution and Command + 2 to decrease it.

- Use Command + 3 to enable triplet grid and Command + 4 to toggle the grid on/off.

6. What function does the Zooming Hotspot serve? How can we open/close it quickly?

- The Zooming Hotspot is the small area at the top of the timeline that allows quick zooming by clicking and dragging vertically or horizontally.
- Open/close it by hovering near the top of the timeline or using Z to zoom in on a selection.

7. What are the methods of zooming horizontally and vertically in Ableton?

- Horizontally: Use H to zoom out to full view and Shift + Scroll for finer control.
- Vertically: Use W to fit all tracks vertically or Alt + Scroll to adjust track heights.

8. How to navigate between clips in Ableton efficiently?

- Use Arrow keys to move between clips in the Session View.
- In the Arrangement View, use Page Up/Page Down or Shift + Tab for fast navigation.

9. What are the different ways in which we copy a clip in Ableton?

- Press Command + C to copy and Command + V to paste.
- Hold Option and drag the clip to duplicate it.
- Use Duplicate with Command + D for quick repetition.

10. How do we Duplicate Clips in Ableton?

- Select a clip and press Command + D to duplicate it immediately, placing an identical clip right after the original.

11. How do we Resize clips in Ableton?

- Drag the clip's edge horizontally to resize, or use the Clip View's Loop Brace for precise length adjustments.

12. How can we loop clips in Ableton?

- Press Command + L after selecting a clip to activate looping.
- Use the Loop Switch in the Clip View to enable or disable loops.

13. How to select tracks and minimize/maximize them quickly in Ableton?

- Select Multiple Tracks: Hold Shift and click.
- Minimize/Maximize: Press Alt + U to toggle track heights efficiently.

14. What is the function of the I/O section in Ableton and how can we show/hide it quickly?

- The I/O section manages track inputs and outputs.
- Show/hide it by pressing Command + I or using the View Menu.

15. What is the function of the Mixer section in Ableton and how can we show/hide it quickly?

- The Mixer section controls volume, panning, and sends for each track.
- Show/hide it with Command + M or through the View Menu.

16. How can mute/unmute tracks in Ableton?

- Press 0 after selecting a track or use the M button in the Mixer to mute/ unmute tracks.

17. What are the methods in which we can change track volume in Ableton?

- Drag the Volume Fader in the Mixer, or adjust in the Track Header.
- Use automation envelopes in the Arrangement View.

18. What is Panning and how do we Pan tracks in Ableton?

- Panning shifts the audio signal left or right in the stereo field.
- Adjust the Pan knob in the Mixer or Track Header for each track.

19. How can we change Zoom Display value in Ableton and what does it change?

- Change the Zoom Display in Preferences > Look/Feel to adjust the size of the interface elements for better visibility.

20. How can we change themes in Ableton?

- Go to Preferences > Look/Feel and select from available themes (Light, Dark, Mid Grey).

21. How can we change the look and feel of Ableton using preferences?

- In Preferences > Look/Feel, modify colour themes, grid line intensity, and zoom levels to personalise the interface.

22. How can we change Grid Line Intensity in Ableton?

- Navigate to Preferences > Look/Feel and use the Grid Line Intensity slider to adjust the brightness of grid lines for better visibility.

23. How can we return the Playhead to the beginning of the session in Ableton?

- Press Shift + Space to return the Playhead to the beginning and start playback.
- Alternatively, press Home on your keyboard, or click the Stop button twice in the Transport Controls to bring the Playhead back to the start.

24. Where can we find Samples in the Ableton Browser?

- Open the Browser (press Command + Option + B).
- Click on Samples in the Categories section, where all installed and imported samples are listed.

- You can also find user-added samples in the User Library under the Places section.

25. Add 3 more drum sounds into the same collection and remove the previous kick from that group.

- In the Browser, locate the drum sounds you want to add.
- Right-click each sound and select Add to Collection, then choose the same collection as the existing group.
- To remove the previous kick, right-click the kick sample in the collection and choose Remove from Collection.

26. Select a kick sample from your browser window and add it to a collection.

- Open the Browser, navigate to Samples > Drums > Kicks.
- Right-click the desired kick sample and select Add to Collection.
- Choose a collection (e.g., Drums, Favourite Kicks), and it will be added for easy access.

27. Insert 4 tracks and colour them differently. Add a sample to each track by dragging it from your browser window.

- Press Command + T to add an audio track. Repeat to create 4 tracks.
- Right-click each track header, select Rename/Color, and choose different colours.
- Drag samples from the Browser into each track, assigning a unique sample to each.

28. Make a new folder on your desktop. Give it a name and add that folder to Ableton's Browser.

- Create a folder on your desktop (e.g., My Samples).
- In Ableton, click Add Folder in the Places section of the Browser.
- Select your new folder, and it will appear in the Browser for quick access.

29. Activate the Metronome in Ableton Live but change the settings of the rhythm of the click to play in triplets.

- Click the Metronome icon in the top bar to activate it.
- Right-click the Metronome icon and select Triplet Grid, changing the click rhythm to triplets.

30. Open a new project. Add 3 audio tracks. Solo one of them. Mute one of them and minimize the other. Save the project with a desired name.

- File > New Live Set.
- Press Command + T three times to add 3 audio tracks.
- Click the S button on one track to solo it, the M button on another to mute it, and click the small arrow on the last track to minimize it.
- File > Save Live Set As..., and enter your desired project name.

31. Open a new project. Add a key mapping to the Follow button on the Letter F. To the recording button R and T to the tap tempo button. Then save it as the default opening window for live.

- Open a new project via File > New Live Set.
- Press Command + K to open Key Mapping mode.
- Click the Follow button and press F, click the Record button and press R, and click the Tap Tempo button and press T.
- Exit Key Mapping mode by pressing Command + K again.
- Go to Preferences > File/Folder > Save Current Set as Default to keep this setup as the default project.

FOUR

Recording Audio in Logic

1. Describe the signal flow from the source of sound to the speakers while recording audio.

- The signal flow during audio recording in Logic Pro follows these steps:

  - Source of Sound: An instrument, microphone, or line-level device produces an audio signal.
  - Microphone/Instrument Cable: Transmits the analog signal to an audio interface.
  - Audio Interface Preamp: Boosts the signal to a usable level (gain staging starts here).
  - Analog-to-Digital Converter (ADC): Converts the analog signal into digital data.
  - Logic Pro DAW: Captures the digital signal on an audio track, where it can be processed with effects, EQ, and mixing tools.
  - Digital-to-Analog Converter (DAC): Converts the processed digital signal back to analog.
  - Speakers/Headphones: Play the final audio signal for monitoring or playback.

2. Explain what you understand by the term gain staging.

- Gain staging refers to managing the levels of an audio signal throughout the recording and mixing process to prevent distortion or noise.

- ○ It begins at the sound source (e.g., instrument level), continues through the preamp (where the signal is boosted), and passes through each stage (such as plugins and the DAW mixer) until the final output.
- ○ Proper gain staging ensures a clean signal by maintaining optimal levels without introducing noise or clipping.

3. What does the quality of your audio signal depend on?

- The quality of an audio signal depends on several factors:

  - ○ Sample Rate: Higher sample rates (e.g., 48kHz, 96kHz) capture more detail.
  - ○ Bit Depth: Higher bit depths (e.g., 24-bit) provide greater dynamic range.
  - ○ Gain Staging: Proper level management prevents distortion.
  - ○ Noise Floor: Lower noise floor means less background noise.
  - ○ Signal-to-Noise Ratio (SNR): Higher SNR ensures a clearer sound by reducing unwanted noise.
  - ○ Equipment Quality: High-quality microphones, cables, and interfaces contribute significantly to sound clarity.

4. Explain what you understand by the terms noise floor and signal-to-noise ratio.

- Noise Floor: The baseline level of background noise in a recording system. All systems generate a small amount of noise, and the goal is to keep it as low as possible.
- Signal-to-Noise Ratio (SNR): The ratio between the audio signal level and the noise floor. A higher SNR means the signal is much louder than the noise, resulting in cleaner audio.

5. How do you change sample rate in Logic?

- Go to Logic Pro > Preferences > Audio > Devices.
- Under Core Audio Settings, select your desired Sample Rate from the dropdown menu.
- Logic will adjust the session's sample rate, but all imported audio must match or be converted.

6. Explain if we can use two different audio samples having different sample rates in the same project.

- Yes, Logic Pro allows the use of samples with different sample rates.

  - When imported, Logic converts audio files to the project's set sample rate to ensure consistency, avoiding pitch shifts or timing errors.

7. What do you understand by the term bit-depth? Can we use two audio samples having different bit-depths in the same project?

- Bit-depth determines the dynamic range of digital audio. For example, 16-bit offers 65,536 amplitude levels, while 24-bit offers over 16 million, providing greater detail and dynamic range.
- Yes, Logic Pro can handle different bit depths by converting them to the project's set bit depth, ensuring consistent quality across all audio files.

8. What is the standard sample rate for Audio and Video files?

- Audio Files: The standard sample rate is 44.1kHz (used for CDs) and 48kHz (commonly used in digital audio workstations and professional audio production).
- Video Files: The standard sample rate is 48kHz for broadcast and film production, ensuring synchronisation with video frames.

9. What do you understand by the term headroom?

- Headroom refers to the amount of available space between the highest peak of an audio signal and the point of digital clipping (0 dBFS).

  - More headroom allows for dynamic peaks without distortion, essential during recording and mixing.

10. What steps can you take to ensure more headroom? What are the benefits of having extra headroom?

- Steps:

- ◦ Lower input gain during recording.
- ◦ Avoid pushing track faders too high in the mixer.
- ◦ Use compressors or limiters to control peaks.
- ◦ Maintain output levels below -6 dBFS during mixing.

- Benefits:

  - ◦ Prevents clipping and distortion.
  - ◦ Provides flexibility during mixing and mastering.
  - ◦ Ensures better sound quality and dynamic range.

11. How do you set your sample rate and bit-depth in Logic?

- Go to Logic Pro > Preferences > Audio > Devices.
- Set the Sample Rate under Core Audio.
- Go to File > Project Settings > Audio, and set the Bit Depth (16-bit, 24-bit, or 32-bit float).

12. Explain the two types of settings that exist in Logic.

- Global Settings: Affect the entire Logic Pro environment (e.g., audio interface setup, MIDI preferences).
- Project Settings: Specific to the current project (e.g., tempo, sample rate, key signature).

13. What do you understand by the term dynamics?

- Dynamics refers to the variation in loudness between the quietest and loudest parts of an audio signal.

  - ◦ Controlling dynamics is crucial in mixing, often achieved using compressors, limiters, and expanders.

14. What do you understand by input and output devices?

- Input Devices: Capture audio signals (e.g., microphones, MIDI controllers, audio interfaces).

- Output Devices: Play back audio (e.g., speakers, headphones, audio interfaces).

15. What are single take recordings?

- A single take recording captures an entire performance in one continuous recording session without stops or edits, often valued for its authenticity and natural feel.

16. What does the record enable and input monitoring buttons do in Logic?

- Record Enable (R): Arms a track for recording, allowing it to capture audio when recording starts.
- Input Monitoring (I): Allows you to hear the audio signal through Logic before recording, useful for monitoring during live performances.

17. Explain what happens when you delete an audio region from a project in Logic.

- Deleting an audio region from the project removes it from the timeline, but the original audio file remains in the Project Audio Browser unless permanently deleted from the project folder.

18. How do you bring a deleted audio region to its original recording position in Logic?

- Open the Project Audio Browser (press F).
- Locate the deleted region, right-click, and choose Place at Original Recording Position.
- Logic will restore the region to its exact spot on the timeline where it was originally recorded.

19. Explain what you understand by the following terms: i) Count-in, ii) Count-in Settings, iii) Metronome, iv) Metronome settings.

- Count-in: A pre-roll of beats that plays before recording starts, helping musicians prepare for the first note.

- Count-in Settings: Adjusted in Record > Recording Settings, where you can set the number of bars for the count-in (e.g., 1 bar, 2 bars).
- Metronome: An audible click that plays at the project's tempo to keep timing consistent during recording and playback.
- Metronome Settings: Found under Logic Pro > Preferences > Metronome, allowing you to change the sound, enable/disable during recording/playback, and set accents for the first beat of each bar.

20. In practice, how much headroom should we save from the beginning of the project to be safe?

- It is recommended to leave at least 6 dB of headroom during recording and mixing.
- Keeping peak levels around -6 dBFS ensures that sudden dynamic peaks don't cause clipping, while still maintaining sufficient signal strength.

21. How do you record additional takes into Logic? How can you create take folders in Logic?

- To record multiple takes, enable Cycle Recording by pressing C and looping a section.
- Each pass creates a new take, automatically placed in a Take Folder.
- You can also manually create a take folder by selecting multiple regions, right-clicking, and choosing Pack Take Folder.

22. Explain what you understand by Punch recording. How can you accomplish it in Logic?

- Punch recording allows you to record over a specific section without affecting the rest of the track.
- Enable it by clicking the Punch In/Out button in the control bar or setting punch points in the Tracks Area by dragging the punch region while in the Cycle area.
- Alternatively, use Auto-Punch for precise in/out points.

23. What is the shortcut to record toggle?

- The shortcut is R to start and stop recording.

24. What is Auto-punch? What are the various methods by which you can accomplish it in Logic?

- Auto-punch records within a specified section while playing back the entire project.
- Methods:

  - Enable Auto-Punch by clicking the red bar in the control bar.
  - Drag the Auto-Punch area in the Tracks Area.
  - Set points in the Control Bar > Customize Control Bar and enable Auto-Punch.

25. How do you choose the recording file-type in Logic?

- Go to File > Project Settings > Recording.
- Choose between AIFF, WAV, or CAF formats under the Audio Recording File Type dropdown.

26. What file format is recommended for recording audio at its best fidelity?

- WAV is recommended due to its uncompressed, high-quality audio and broad compatibility.

27. How do we delete unused samples from a project in Logic and what can be the benefits of such action?

- Open the Project Audio Browser (F), select unused files, and choose Delete Unused.
- Benefits:

  - Reduces project size.
  - Prevents clutter in the session.
  - Improves project load times and overall performance.

28. How do you activate Division metronome? How can you play it in triplets in a project with the time signature 4/4?

- Go to LCD Display > Custom > Metronome Settings.
- Enable Division for a subdivided metronome click.
- To play in triplets, adjust the Division value to Triplets in the metronome settings.

29. Where can you find the sample rate settings in Logic?

- Found under Logic Pro > Preferences > Audio > Devices > Sample Rate dropdown.

30. What precaution must you take before record-enabling multiple tracks simultaneously in Logic?

- Ensure that the disk I/O buffer size is set high (e.g., 256 or 512 samples) to prevent audio dropouts.
- Check that your audio interface can handle multiple inputs simultaneously without latency issues.

31. In Autopunch mode, how do you set punch-in and punch-out points in Logic?

- Enable Autopunch and drag the red bar in the Tracks Area to set punch-in and punch-out points.
- Alternatively, use the Locators in the ruler to set the range.

32. Describe an easy way to access your Count-in Settings.

- Right-click the Record button in the Transport Bar and select Recording Settings, where you can adjust the Count-in bars and metronome preferences.

33. What happens when you raise the I/O buffer size?

- Increasing the I/O buffer size reduces CPU load and latency issues but increases overall latency, suitable for mixing.
- Lowering it minimizes latency, ideal for recording but increases CPU load.

34. In the "project file browser", when you select unused files, what determines whether a file is used or unused?

- Used files are highlighted and show a reference count in the session.
- Unused files appear greyed out with no reference count, indicating they are not part of the current project timeline.

FIVE
RECORDING AUDIO IN ABLETON

1. How do we set up recording in Ableton?

- Open Preferences (Command + ,) and go to Audio.
- Select your Audio Interface as the Input and Output device.
- Create a new Audio Track (Command + T).
- In the track's I/O section, choose the correct Input channel from your interface.
- Click the Arm Recording button on the track, then press Record (F9) to start recording.

2. How can we change our recording file type?

- Go to Preferences > Record/Warp/Launch.
- Under File Type, select either WAV or AIFF, both offering high-quality, uncompressed audio suitable for professional recording.

3. How can we change the recording Sample Rate?

- Open Preferences > Audio.
- Set the Sample Rate in the In/Out Sample Rate dropdown (e.g., 44.1kHz for standard audio, 48kHz for video, or higher for detailed recordings).

4. What is Default SR/Pitch Conversion and what is the best setting for it?

- Sample Rate (SR)/Pitch Conversion ensures correct audio playback when samples are at different sample rates.
- Best setting: Use High Quality to maintain audio fidelity, although this may increase CPU load.

5. How can we change the Bit-depth of our recording?

- Go to Preferences > Record/Warp/Launch.
- Choose the Bit Depth (16-bit for CDs, 24-bit for better dynamic range, or 32-bit float for maximum flexibility).

6. How can we select our audio driver in Ableton?

- In Preferences > Audio, choose your audio driver under Driver Type (e.g., CoreAudio for Mac, ASIO for Windows).
- Select your Audio Device from the dropdown.

7. How do we set up Inputs and Outputs for recording audio in Ableton?

- In Preferences > Audio > Input Config/Output Config, enable the necessary input/output channels from your audio interface.
- In each track's I/O section, choose the appropriate input/output routing.

8. How can input signal from a microphone into Ableton?

- Connect the microphone to your audio interface.
- Create an Audio Track (Command + T).
- In the track's I/O section, select the microphone's input channel.
- Click Arm Recording, and you will see the input signal in the track meter.

9. How do we change Channel Configuration in Ableton?

- In Preferences > Audio > Input Config/Output Config, enable or disable Mono and Stereo channels based on your input needs.

10. What are the different Input Monitoring modes we use during recording and explain how they function?

- Off: No input monitoring through Ableton, but the signal is still recorded.
- Auto: Monitors input only when recording is enabled or when playback is stopped.
- In: Continuously monitors the input signal, even during playback.

11. How to arm tracks for recording? How can we arm multiple tracks?

- Click the Arm Recording button (red circle) on each track.
- To arm multiple tracks simultaneously, hold Shift while clicking the Arm button on multiple tracks.

12. What is the role of the Exclusive function in Ableton?

- Exclusive Arm/Solo ensures that only one track is armed or soloed at a time, avoiding accidental multi-track recording.
- Enable it in Preferences > Record/Warp/Launch by checking Exclusive Arm or Exclusive Solo.

13. How to set Punch In and Punch Out recording in Ableton?

- Enable Punch In/Out buttons in the Control Bar.
- Set the start and end points in the Arrangement View timeline.
- Punch recording starts and stops automatically within the set range.

14. How can we create Take folders in Ableton? Mention 2 ways.

- Method 1: Enable Loop Recording in the Arrangement View; each pass creates a new take stacked together.
- Method 2: Manually Group clips by selecting multiple takes, right-clicking, and choosing Group Tracks, which acts as a take folder.

15. What is comping and how do we do it in Ableton?

- Comping is the process of selecting the best parts from multiple recorded takes to create a single, polished performance.
- In Ableton Live 11 or later, record multiple takes, click the track header, and choose Show Take Lanes.

- Use the Draw Tool (B) to select the best segments from each take, which composes the final version.

16. How can we open take folders quickly in Ableton?

- In Arrangement View, enable Loop Recording by clicking the Loop button in the Control Bar and setting loop points.
- Each looped recording creates a new take lane, which you can access by right-clicking the track and selecting Show Take Lanes.
- Alternatively, group multiple clips into a take folder by selecting them, right-clicking, and choosing Group Tracks.

17. What is Count-in and how can we set it in Ableton?

- Count-in provides a metronome click before recording starts, allowing performers to prepare.
- Set it by clicking the Metronome icon and choosing the count-in length (e.g., 1 bar, 2 bars) from the dropdown menu.

18. How can we access Metronome controls in Ableton?

- Right-click the Metronome icon in the Control Bar to access settings like Sound, Count-in, and Enable/Disable during playback or recording.

19. How can we change the tone of the Metronome and what purpose does it serve?

- Right-click the Metronome icon and choose from different Sound Presets (e.g., Classic, Click, Wood).
- Changing the tone ensures the metronome is clearly audible, even in complex sessions with many instruments.

20. How can we control Metronome volume in Ableton?

- Click the small arrow next to the Metronome icon to open the Cue Out section in the mixer.
- Adjust the Cue Volume knob to control metronome loudness independently from the main mix.

21. How can we automatically turn Metronome on while Recording and off when the recording is complete?

- In Preferences > Record/Warp/Launch, enable Metronome during Recording but disable Metronome during Playback.

22. How can we open clip properties in Ableton?

- Double-click any clip to open its properties in the Clip View at the bottom of the screen.

23. What information can we access from Clip Properties?

- Warp settings, Loop start/end points, Pitch transposition, Gain adjustments, and Envelope automation.

24. What is the use of RAM and HI-Q buttons in Ableton?

- RAM Button: Loads the clip into RAM for faster playback, reducing strain on the hard drive.
- HI-Q Button: Enables high-quality sample rate conversion, ensuring better audio fidelity when pitch-shifting or time-stretching.

25. Where and how can we change Buffer Size in Ableton and what effect does it have on the DAW?

- Go to Preferences > Audio > Buffer Size.
- Lower buffer sizes reduce latency but increase CPU load, while higher buffer sizes reduce CPU usage but increase latency.

26. What is Latency?

- Latency is the delay between inputting audio (e.g., playing a guitar) and hearing the output.
- It occurs due to the time needed for analog-to-digital conversion, processing, and digital-to-analog conversion.

27. What is Direct Monitoring? Why is it used?

- Direct Monitoring sends input signals directly to the output without passing through the DAW, reducing latency during recording.

28. What is the role of Driver Error Compensation?

- It corrects timing inaccuracies caused by audio drivers, ensuring recorded audio aligns perfectly with the timeline.

29. Where can we activate automatic Delay Compensation and Reduced Latency When Monitoring? How do these options help us?

- In Preferences > Audio, enable Delay Compensation and Reduced Latency When Monitoring.
- They ensure accurate playback timing and minimise latency during live recording.

30. What is Track Delay? How can you add Track Delay in Ableton?

- Track Delay offsets a track's timing by milliseconds to correct latency or timing issues.
- Add it by enabling Track Delay in the mixer and entering the delay amount.

31. How can we export or render files in Ableton?

- Go to File > Export Audio/Video, choose the desired format (WAV, MP3), and set options like bit depth and sample rate.

32. While exporting what are the considerations we should take for optimum results?

- Use WAV at 24-bit/48kHz, enable Dither for bit depth reduction, and ensure Normalize is off for unaltered dynamics.

33. What is PCM?

- Pulse Code Modulation (PCM) is a digital representation of analog audio, used in WAV and AIFF formats for lossless recording.

34. How can we export in WAV or MP3 in Ableton?

- In File > Export Audio/Video, select WAV or MP3 as the file type, then adjust quality settings before exporting.

35. Open a new project in Live. Go to the audio tab under preferences and write how you would set up Ableton in a way that it receives input from an audio interface but outputs out of your laptop.

- In Preferences > Audio, select the Audio Interface as the Input Device and the Built-in Output as the Output Device.

36. Open a project in Ableton. Set up a track in such a way that it starts recording audio from the arrangement position 4.1.1 and stops after two bars.

- Set the Start Marker at 4.1.1.
- Enable Punch In at 4.1.1 and Punch Out at 6.1.1 (two bars later) in the timeline.

SIX
Editing Audio in Logic

1. What do you understand by audio editing?

- Audio editing refers to the process of manipulating recorded audio to enhance its quality, structure, and overall impact. It includes tasks such as cutting, trimming, adjusting volume levels, adding effects, and arranging audio segments within a project. In Logic Pro, audio editing can be performed non-destructively, ensuring the original recordings remain intact while allowing for extensive modifications.

2. What do you understand by the term zero-crossing?

- Zero-crossing refers to the point where an audio waveform crosses the zero amplitude line. Editing at zero-crossings ensures that audio cuts or edits occur where the waveform intersects the zero line, reducing the likelihood of unwanted clicks or pops. Logic Pro's Zero Crossing Edit mode ensures smooth transitions between edited regions by automatically aligning cuts at zero-crossing points.

3. Where in Logic can you perform non-destructive and destructive editing?

- Non-destructive Editing:

  - Performed in the Tracks Area or Audio Editor.

○ Edits such as fades, trims, and volume adjustments do not alter the original audio file.

• Destructive Editing:

○ Performed in the File Editor (press W to open).
○ Actions like normalizing, reversing, or permanently deleting audio are applied directly to the original audio file, altering it irreversibly.

4. What are all the tools you have access to in Logic? What do you understand by Left-click tool and Command-click tool?

• Tools in Logic Pro include:

○ Pointer Tool: For selecting and moving regions.
○ Marquee Tool: For selecting and editing specific parts of regions.
○ Fade Tool: For creating fade-ins and fade-outs.
○ Scissors Tool: For cutting regions.
○ Zoom Tool: For zooming into the timeline.
○ Flex Tool: For time-stretching and pitch-shifting audio.

• Left-click Tool: The default tool activated when using the left mouse button.
• Command-click Tool: An additional tool activated by holding the Command key while clicking, allowing quick access to a secondary tool without changing the primary one.

5. What are the various uses of the Marquee tool?

• The Marquee Tool is versatile and essential for audio editing in Logic Pro. It allows users to:

○ Select specific portions of an audio region for editing.
○ Cut, copy, or move selected sections without affecting the rest of the region.
○ Create fades quickly by dragging the edges of a selection.
○ Loop specific sections by selecting and pressing L.

- ◦ Apply processing such as gain changes or effects to the selected area only.

6. How do you colour regions in Logic?

- Select the desired region in the Tracks Area.
- Press Option + C to open the Colour Palette.
- Choose a colour to apply to the selected region, helping to visually organise tracks and differentiate between various sections.

7. What are clicks and pops? Why are they produced? How can we remove them?

- Clicks and pops are unwanted audio artifacts caused by abrupt waveform transitions, improper edits, or digital errors.
- They are often produced when cutting audio at non-zero crossing points or due to sample rate mismatches.
- Removal Methods:

  - ◦ Use the Fade Tool to create short fade-ins and fade-outs at edit points.
  - ◦ Enable Snap to Zero Crossing in the Audio Editor.
  - ◦ Apply the De-clicking plugin in Logic's Audio FX.

8. Define the following:

- Fades: Gradual increase or decrease in audio volume.
- Fade-in: Audio gradually increases from silence to full volume.
- Fade-out: Audio gradually decreases from full volume to silence.
- Crossfade: Smooth transition between two overlapping audio regions by fading one out while fading the other in.
- Equal Powered Crossfade: Maintains consistent volume during the crossfade by applying equal gain to both regions.
- Batch Fades: Applying fades to multiple regions simultaneously, saving time during large projects.

9. How can you add curves to your fades?

- Select the fade by clicking on its fade line in the Tracks Area.

- Drag the fade curve handle (a small dot on the fade line) to adjust the shape, creating linear, exponential, or logarithmic fade curves for smoother or more dramatic transitions.

10. How can you use speed-up/slow-down effects or turntable effects in Logic?

- Open the Flex Tool and enable Flex Time for the track.
- Use the Speed tool (located within the Flex Tool menu) to stretch or compress audio regions, creating speed-up or slow-down effects.
- Alternatively, apply the Varispeed function in the Control Bar, which emulates turntable pitch manipulation by altering the entire project's tempo and pitch dynamically.

11. What do you understand by the term Transients?

- Transients are short bursts of high energy at the beginning of an audio signal, such as the initial hit of a drum or the pluck of a guitar string. They help define the attack and rhythm in music and are crucial for tasks like drum replacement, timing adjustments, and dynamic processing in Logic Pro.

12. What do you understand by the term ADSR?

- ADSR stands for Attack, Decay, Sustain, and Release, which are the four stages of an audio signal's envelope:

  - Attack: Time taken for the sound to reach peak level after a note is played.
  - Decay: Time for the sound to reduce to the sustain level after the initial peak.
  - Sustain: The level at which the sound remains while the note is held.
  - Release: Time for the sound to fade out after the note is released.

- ADSR is commonly used in Logic's Sampler and Synthesizer instruments for shaping sound dynamics.

13. What is Snapping? Define what does snap to absolute values and snap to relative values stand for in Logic.

- Snapping aligns regions, notes, or automation points to the grid in the Tracks Area.
- Snap to Absolute Values: Positions items directly to the nearest grid line.
- Snap to Relative Values: Maintains the relative position of an item while aligning it to the grid.

14. How can you turn on Alignment Guides in Logic? What are its uses?

- Enable Alignment Guides in Logic Pro > Preferences > Editing.
- Guides appear as lines to help align regions, markers, and automation, ensuring precise editing and avoiding timing errors.

15. What do you understand by Phase?

- Phase refers to the alignment of audio waveforms. When waveforms are in phase, their peaks and troughs align, producing a stronger signal. When out of phase, they can cancel each other out, causing a weaker or silent signal.

16. What will happen if two identical waveforms, in phase, are played together? What will happen if one of them is inverted?

- In Phase: The waveforms reinforce each other, increasing the amplitude.
- Inverted Phase: The waveforms cancel each other out, resulting in silence due to phase cancellation.

17. What do you understand by Phase Inversion and how can you achieve it in Logic?

- Phase Inversion flips the polarity of an audio signal, effectively reversing the waveform.
- In Logic, apply Phase Inversion using the Gain plugin under Audio FX > Utility > Gain and enable Phase Invert Left/Right.

18. How do you Comp in Logic?

- Comping is combining the best parts of multiple takes into one final take:
- Record several takes in a Take Folder.
- Click and drag over sections in different takes to select the best parts, automatically creating a comp track.

19. Demonstrate how you can remove auto-crossfades during the comping process?

- Select the Take Folder.
- Open the Inspector (I) and deselect "Crossfade" under the Take Folder options, removing all automatic crossfades.

20. What is quick-swipe comping?

- Quick-swipe comping is a feature in Logic that allows seamless selection of the best sections from multiple takes by simply clicking and dragging over regions in a take folder, instantly creating a composite take.

21. What command can you use to move regions very precisely?

- Hold Shift + Option while dragging a region to move it in fine increments or adjust the Nudge value in the toolbar and use the Nudge Left/Right keys (< and >).

22. How do you import audio into Logic?

- Drag an audio file directly into the Tracks Area from the Finder.
- Or use File > Import > Audio File... and choose the desired file.

23. What function does the sample editor serve in Logic?

- The Sample Editor allows for detailed waveform editing, including:
- Cutting, Fading, Normalizing, Reversing, and Time-Stretching audio at the sample level.

24. What is the Track editor and what are the benefits of using it?

- The Track Editor provides a focused view of a selected track for detailed region editing, automation, and pitch correction without zooming in the main timeline.

25. What purpose does the file editor serve in Logic?

- The File Editor performs destructive edits such as trimming, applying effects, and converting formats directly on the audio file.

26. How do you use the anchor tool in Logic? Where is it Located?

- The Anchor Tool is located in the Audio File Editor.
- It sets the reference point in an audio region, aligning that point to the grid when dragging the region.

27. How can you reverse audio files in Logic?

- Select an audio region, open the File Editor (W), and choose Functions > Reverse to flip the audio backward.

28. What is the shortcut of the pickup clock?

- Press Shift + Command + R to move the selected region to the current playhead position, known as the Pickup Clock.

29. What do you understand by scrubbing? What is it used for and How can accomplish scrubbing in Logic?

- Scrubbing plays audio as you drag the playhead, useful for precise edits and locating transients.
- Enable it by pressing Shift + Space or using the Scrub Tool from the toolbar.

30. What are the shortcuts to the following:

- Pointer Tool: T + 1
- Left-click Tool: T + 1
- Fade Tool: T + 4

- Pencil Tool: T + 2
- Mute: Control + M
- Solo: S

31. Can you cut a region into multiple smaller regions using the scissor tool? If yes, demonstrate how. Also explain what will determine the size of each dissected region.

- Yes, select the Scissors Tool (T + 3).
- Hold Option and click where you want the first cut, and Logic will automatically divide the region into equal segments based on the grid setting or the length between the original click and the next grid line.

32. What do you understand by the term glitch?

- A glitch refers to an unintended, often sudden audio artifact caused by digital errors, buffer underruns, or incomplete data processing. In music production, glitches can either be problematic or used creatively as glitch effects to add texture and rhythmic interest to tracks.

33. What are digital artefacts?

- Digital artefacts are unwanted byproducts of digital audio processing, such as aliasing, clipping, quantization noise, or poor sample rate conversion. They often degrade audio quality and occur when working with compressed files, low bit depths, or incorrect processing settings.

34. How do you stutter a region in Logic?

- Select the audio region and use the Scissors Tool (T + 3) to make multiple small cuts.
- Duplicate the cuts using Option + Drag.
- Adjust the timing using the Nudge Tool or apply a Repeat Section using Command + R to create rhythmic stutter effects.

35. How can you bounce regions in place in Logic?

- Select the region(s) you want to bounce.

- Right-click and choose Bounce in Place (Control + B).
- Logic creates a new audio file from the selected region, embedding all applied effects and edits.

36. How can we remove the M and S buttons or the R and I buttons from the track header in Logic and how can you bring it back?

- Go to Logic Pro > Preferences > Display > Tracks.
- Uncheck Mute (M), Solo (S), Record (R), or Input Monitoring (I) to remove them.
- To bring them back, recheck these options under the same preferences menu.

37. Explain what you understand by the following Drag settings:

- Overlap: Overlapping regions are placed on top of each other without splitting.
- No-overlap: Automatically splits regions where they overlap.
- X-fade: Applies automatic crossfades between overlapping regions.
- Shuffle L: Moves regions left automatically, filling any gaps.
- Shuffle R: Moves regions right automatically, aligning with the next region.

38. What is the function of "go to position" in Logic and what are its uses?

- Go to Position (Option + P) allows you to navigate directly to a specific bar, beat, or timecode in your project, ensuring precise placement and editing during large sessions.

39. What is nudge value? How can you nudge a region by 1 ms?

- Nudge value determines how far a region moves when nudged.
- Set it by clicking the Nudge Value dropdown in the Toolbar and selecting 1 ms.
- Nudge a region using the Left/Right Arrow keys with the selected nudge value.

40. What is the shortcut for nudging?

- Comma (,) to nudge left and Period (.) to nudge right.

41. How can we move a selected region to a selected track? Why is it necessary?

- Select the region and press Option + Shift + Down/Up Arrow to move it to the selected track.
- This is necessary for organising, layering, and mixing without disrupting timing or alignment.

42. How do you edit files transient to transient by using keyboard shortcuts?

- Enable Flex Mode and press Shift + Tab to jump from one transient to the next for precise editing, trimming, and quantizing.

43. How can we trim regions by using the nudge function?

- Select the region edge, hold Shift, and use the Comma (,) or Period (.) keys to trim in small increments based on the Nudge Value.

44. Is it possible to use the marquee tool to select a region inside a region? How can you move your marquee selection from transient to transient in Logic?

- Yes, use the Marquee Tool to select any part inside a larger region.
- To move the marquee selection transient to transient, press Shift + Tab while using the Marquee Tool, allowing for precise edits aligned to transients.

45. In a region marked by a marquee, how do you select the next hit in the region in Logic using keyboard shortcuts?

- After marking a region with the Marquee Tool, press Tab to jump to the next transient or hit within the selected region. This allows for precise editing, particularly when working with rhythmic material like drums or percussive elements.

46. How can we edit a file recorded with multiple mics in Logic?

- Group the tracks by selecting all mic recordings, right-clicking, and choosing Create Track Group.
- Enable Phase-Locked Editing in the Group Settings to ensure edits apply simultaneously to all tracks, maintaining phase alignment.
- Use tools like Flex Time for timing corrections or Strip Silence for removing unwanted noise across all mic tracks.

47. What is the purpose of the function of Strip Silence in Logic?

- Strip Silence automatically removes sections of silence from audio recordings, leaving only the portions with sound.
- Access it via Audio > Strip Silence from Audio Region.
- It's particularly useful for cleaning up drum recordings or dialogue by removing noise between hits or phrases.

48. How can we split a region or region using the playhead or Locator?

- Place the Playhead at the desired point in the timeline.
- Press Command + T to split the selected region at the playhead position.
- Alternatively, use Locators to define a range and press Control + Command + T to split the region within the Locator boundaries.

49. How can you insert silence in your arrangement in Logic?

- Select the region or area in the Tracks Area.
- Press Command + Shift + Z to insert silence, which shifts all following regions to the right by the selected amount of time.

50. Explain the purpose of the Musical Grid in Logic.

- The Musical Grid aligns regions, notes, and automation to musical time (bars, beats) instead of absolute time, ensuring that edits stay rhythmically accurate.
- Grid settings like Snap to Grid or Smart Snap help in maintaining tempo and timing integrity during editing and arranging.

51. How do you add a fade-in and fade-out in a region?

- Hover over the top-left or top-right corner of an audio region until the Fade Tool appears.
- Drag inward to create a Fade-in or Fade-out.
- Alternatively, select the region and apply fades using the Region Inspector (I) by adjusting the Fade In/Out parameters.

52. How do you add a crossfade between two regions?

- Overlap two audio regions slightly.
- Select both regions, right-click, and choose Crossfade > Create Crossfade (X).
- Adjust the length of the crossfade by dragging the fade handles.

53. How do you curve your fades in Logic?

- After creating a fade, click the fade line to reveal the Fade Curve handle.
- Drag the handle up or down to adjust the curve, altering the fade's shape from linear to exponential or logarithmic.

54. How do you select a section of an audio region?

- Use the Marquee Tool (T + 3) to click and drag over the desired section within an audio region.
- This selection can then be cut, copied, or edited independently from the rest of the region.

SEVEN

USING FLEX, SMART TEMPO, AND VARISPEED IN LOGIC

1. How do you create vocal harmonies by using flex pitch in Logic?

- Select the vocal region and enable Flex Pitch in the Track Inspector.
- Double-click the region to open the Audio Track Editor.
- Adjust the pitch of selected notes by dragging them to different pitches, creating harmonies (e.g., a third or fifth above the original melody).

2. How can you change the following in flex pitch (explain with examples): i) Gain, ii) Pitch Drift, iii) Vibrato?

- Gain: Adjust the Gain Handle on each pitch segment to increase or decrease volume (e.g., raising gain for softer notes).
- Pitch Drift: Modify the Drift Handle to correct pitch drift at the start or end of a note (e.g., reducing drift for sustained notes).
- Vibrato: Use the Vibrato Handle to add or reduce vibrato (e.g., increasing vibrato for expressive vocal passages).

3. How can you fine-tune vocals by using flex pitch in Logic?

- Enable Flex Pitch and use the Fine Pitch Tool to manually adjust pitch variations, ensuring precise pitch correction without affecting the natural tone of the vocals.

4. Explain the purposes of formant shift in flex pitch in Logic.

- Formant Shift alters the harmonic content of audio without changing pitch, useful for changing the timbre of a voice (e.g., making a vocal sound more masculine or feminine).

5. How do you time correct audio using flex? If yes then demonstrate.

- Enable Flex Time in the Track Inspector.
- Drag transient markers in the Audio Track Editor to adjust the timing of notes or beats, aligning them with the project's tempo grid.

6. Explain what you understand by the following:

- Flex Time - Automatic: Logic detects and applies the best flex mode based on audio content.
- Flex Time - Monophonic: Best for single melodic lines, like vocals or bass.
- Flex Time - Slicing: Maintains transient timing, ideal for drums and percussive elements.
- Flex Time - Rhythmic: Maintains rhythmic integrity for audio with clear beats.
- Flex Time - Polyphonic: Used for complex audio like chords and ensembles.
- Flex Time - Speed(Fx): Changes playback speed without altering pitch.
- Flex Time - Tempophone(Fx): Creates a granular effect by adjusting audio speed with granular synthesis.

7. What algorithm can you use to manipulate percussion audio samples the best?

- Flex Time - Slicing is best for percussion, ensuring that transients remain intact while adjusting timing.

8. Make a comparison between Flex time - Slicing and Flex time - Rhythmic.

- Slicing: Maintains transient positions, perfect for drums and rhythmic loops.
- Rhythmic: Maintains rhythmic flow, ideal for audio with continuous rhythm like guitar strumming.

9. How do you use Flex Time - Speed(Fx) and Tempophone(Fx)?

- Speed(Fx): Adjust playback speed for effects like slow motion or fast-forward.
- Tempophone(Fx): Adds a granular stutter effect by manipulating playback speed with grain repetition.

10. What do you understand by grain size in Flex and how can we manipulate it?

- Grain Size refers to the length of individual grains in granular synthesis.
- Manipulate it in the Tempophone(Fx) mode by adjusting the Grain Size slider, affecting the smoothness or choppiness of the audio.

11. How do you Group tracks in Logic?

- Select multiple tracks, right-click, and choose Create Track Group.
- Access Group Settings to enable options like volume, editing, and phase-locked editing.

12. What is the purpose of Smart Tempo in Logic?

- Smart Tempo synchronizes imported audio to the project tempo or adjusts the project tempo to match the audio, essential for remixing and tempo alignment.

13. What is the purpose of Keep mode?

- Keep Mode in Smart Tempo retains the original tempo of imported audio without applying project tempo adjustments.

14. Can we record something into Logic in a different tempo and have the recording sync to your project tempo? If yes then demonstrate.

- Yes, enable Smart Tempo and select Adapt mode.
- Record your audio, and Logic will automatically sync the recording to the project tempo.

15. Will 3rd party loops sync to logic upon import? Demonstrate with an example.

- Yes, with Smart Tempo enabled.
- Import a loop, and Logic will detect its tempo, offering options to match it to the project tempo automatically.

16. What is the purpose of Adapt Mode in Logic?

- Adapt Mode adjusts the project tempo dynamically to match the tempo of recorded or imported audio, useful for free-tempo recordings.

17. Can we record or import a loop into Logic and have our project tempo be synced with the audio's tempo? If yes then demonstrate. Also explain the benefits of this function.

- Yes, using Adapt Mode in Smart Tempo.
- Benefits include seamless integration of loops with varying tempos and flexibility in tempo adjustments without manual editing.

18. What is the function of Varispeed? Explain a few uses of this function with appropriate examples.

- Varispeed changes the overall tempo and pitch of a project in real-time.
- Uses:

  - Slow down complex sections for editing.
  - Experiment with tempo and pitch for creative effects.
  - Align project speed to external video or audio sources.

19. How can you remix a song in Logic using smart tempo?

- Import the song into Logic with Smart Tempo enabled.
- Use Adapt Mode to match the project tempo to the song.

- Slice, loop, and manipulate sections using Flex Time and Varispeed for a complete remix.

EIGHT
EDITING AUDIO IN ABLETON

1. What are the different classifications under which we can divide editing within Ableton?

- Editing in Ableton can be classified into the following categories:

  ○ Clip Editing: Adjusting individual audio or MIDI clips (e.g., trimming, stretching).
  ○ Arrangement Editing: Editing clips along the timeline (e.g., cutting, moving, consolidating).
  ○ Warp Editing: Time-stretching audio to align with tempo.
  ○ Automation Editing: Adjusting parameters over time (e.g., volume, panning, effects).
  ○ MIDI Editing: Modifying MIDI notes, velocity, and timing within MIDI clips.
  ○ Destructive Editing: Permanent changes made in the Sample Editor.
  ○ Non-destructive Editing: Reversible edits applied within the Session and Arrangement views.

2. How do we perform basic edits within Ableton? Give us as many examples as possible.

- Cutting Clips: Select a clip and press Command + X.
- Copying and Pasting: Use Command + C and Command + V.
- Splitting Clips: Place the cursor and press Command + E.

- Consolidating Clips: Select multiple clips and press Command + J.
- Duplicating: Use Command + D.
- Warping: Enable Warp in the Clip View and adjust Warp Markers to time-stretch.
- Reversing Clips: Press R in the Clip View to reverse audio.
- Activating/Deactivating Clips: Press 0 to toggle clip activation.
- Nudging Clips: Use Arrow keys with Shift for precise movement.
- Looping: Press Command + L to loop selected clips.

3. How do we select multiple clips in Ableton?

- Hold Shift and click on multiple clips in the Session or Arrangement view.
- Or use Command + A to select all clips in a track or area.

4. How do we Split clips in Ableton and what is Batch Split?

- Split Clips: Place the playhead at the desired position and press Command + E.
- Batch Split: Select multiple clips and apply Command + E to split all selected clips simultaneously.

5. How do we Cut in Ableton?

- Select the clip or portion of a clip and press Command + X to cut it, removing it from the timeline and placing it in the clipboard.

6. How can we Copy and Paste clips quickly in Ableton?

- Select the clip, press Command + C to copy, and Command + V to paste it at the playhead position or any selected track.

7. How can we activate/deactivate clips within Ableton?

- Select a clip and press 0 to toggle between activating and deactivating it.
- Deactivated clips do not play back but remain in the project.

8. How do we Reverse clips in Ableton?

- Double-click a clip to open the Clip View, and click the Reverse button to flip the audio or MIDI playback direction.

9. What role does Consolidation play and how do we do it in Ableton?

- Consolidation merges multiple clips into a single clip, simplifying arrangement and editing.
- Select the clips and press Command + J to consolidate them into one continuous clip.

10. What is the difference between destructive and non-destructive editing?

- Destructive Editing: Permanent changes made directly to the audio file (e.g., edits in the Sample Editor).
- Non-destructive Editing: Edits that do not alter the original file, allowing for reversibility (e.g., clip warping, trimming, automation).

11. Give an example of destructive editing.

- Destructive Editing Example: Reversing an audio clip directly in the Sample Editor (Clip View). Once reversed and saved, the original audio file is permanently altered.

12. How do we nudge clips in Ableton?

- Select the clip and use the Left/Right Arrow keys to nudge it by the current grid setting.
- For finer adjustments, hold Shift while using the arrow keys.

13. What is Project Standardization?

- Project Standardization refers to organizing an Ableton project with consistent file management, track naming, color coding, and using templates to maintain workflow efficiency.

14. How can we place project markers and locators within Ableton? Give us an example.

- In Arrangement View, right-click the timeline and choose Add Locator.
- Example: Place locators at sections like Intro, Chorus, and Bridge to navigate quickly during editing or performance.

15. How can we change the level of individual clips within a single track in Ableton?

- Adjust Clip Gain in the Clip View by dragging the Clip Volume Slider, independent of the track's main volume.

16. What is Clip Gain and where is it located?

- Clip Gain controls the volume of a specific audio clip without affecting the entire track.
- Located in the Clip View, near the waveform display.

17. How can we add Fade-in and Fade-out in clips and how can we manipulate their curves?

- Enable fades by clicking the clip's edge in Arrangement View and dragging the fade handles.
- Adjust fade curves by dragging the curve handle in the middle of the fade line.

18. How can we add fades quickly?

- Select a clip and press Command + Option + F to apply a default fade.
- Drag the fade handles for quick adjustments.

19. How do we Crossfade in Ableton?

- Overlap two clips in the Arrangement View, then right-click and choose Create Crossfade.

20. How can we activate/deactivate Create Fades on Clip Edges? What does it do?

- Go to Preferences > Record/Warp/Launch and toggle Create Fades on Clip Edges.
- It automatically applies fades at the start and end of clips to prevent clicks.

21. Explain Ableton's Grid system in detail. Also mention the 4 main shortcuts used for manipulating the Grid.

- Grid System: Aligns clips, notes, and automation to time intervals for precise editing.
- Grid Shortcuts:

  - Command + 1: Increase grid resolution.
  - Command + 2: Decrease grid resolution.
  - Command + 3: Toggle triplet grid.
  - Command + 4: Toggle grid snapping.

22. What is the difference between Fixed Grid and Adaptive Grid in Ableton?

- Fixed Grid: Maintains a constant grid size regardless of zoom level.
- Adaptive Grid: Adjusts grid size dynamically based on zoom level.

23. How can we turn the Grid off in Ableton?

- Press Command + 4 to toggle the grid off.

24. How can we activate Triplet Grid?

- Press Command + 3 to enable triplet grid divisions.

25. What is the difference between basic edits and time-based edits?

- Basic Edits: Include actions like cutting, copying, pasting, and fading.
- Time-Based Edits: Involve adjusting timing, such as warping, quantizing, and time-stretching.

26. How can we Cut Time in Ableton?

- Select a time range in the Arrangement View and press Shift + Command + X to cut the time selection and shift all subsequent clips.

27. How can we Paste Time in Ableton?

- Copy a time selection and press Shift + Command + V to paste it into a new position in the timeline.

28. How can we Duplicate Time in Ableton?

- Select a time range and press Shift + Command + D to duplicate it, including all clips and automation within the selection.

29. What is the difference between regular duplicate and duplicate time?

- Duplicate (Command + D): Copies selected clips directly after the original.
- Duplicate Time (Shift + Command + D): Copies an entire time range, including silence, clips, and automation.

30. How do we Insert Silence in a project?

- Select a time range in Arrangement View and press Command + I to insert silence.

31. How can we change the pitch of any Audio File in Ableton?

- In Clip View, adjust the Transpose knob to raise or lower pitch by semitones.

32. How can we loop a clip just by dragging in Ableton?

- Drag the loop bracket in the Clip View to extend loops or grab the clip's edge while holding Option to loop it in the timeline.

33. How can we change the tempo of a clip from half time to double time?

- Enable Warp, right-click the clip, and choose Halve Tempo or Double Tempo from the Warp menu.

34. What is the function of Segment BPM?

- Displays the detected tempo of a warped clip and allows manual input to correct or adjust its tempo for accurate playback.

35. How can we Phase Invert an audio file?

- Use the Utility plugin from the Audio Effects and enable the Phase Invert button for left, right, or both channels.

36. Explain how stretching a clip can affect its sound. What is the relationship between Pitch and Tempo of a sample?

- Stretching a clip changes its playback speed, affecting both pitch and tempo.
- Traditional stretching: Slowing down reduces pitch, and speeding up increases pitch.
- Warping: Maintains pitch while stretching tempo.

37. What are Warp Modes? Are they an example of destructive or non-destructive editing?

- Warp Modes adjust audio playback in time without altering pitch. Types include Beats, Tones, Texture, Re-Pitch, Complex, and Complex Pro.
- Warp modes are a form of non-destructive editing since the original audio file remains unchanged.

38. Where are the warping controls located in Ableton's Preferences?

- Go to Preferences > Record/Warp/Launch > Warp/Fades for global warp settings.

39. How can we time stretch an imported audio file without using Segment BPM in Ableton?

- Enable Warp in the Clip View.
- Adjust the Warp Markers manually by dragging them along the timeline to stretch the audio without altering the BPM setting.

40. Explain each Warp Mode and their characteristics. Also mention what kind of audio is best suited for which Warp Mode.

- Beats: Preserves transients, ideal for drums and percussion.
- Tones: Best for melodic material with clear pitch, such as vocals or bass.
- Texture: Suitable for complex textures and soundscapes, using adjustable Grain Size and Flux.
- Re-Pitch: Changes pitch when adjusting tempo, similar to vinyl speed adjustments.
- Complex: Suitable for full tracks with mixed elements, balancing quality and CPU usage.
- Complex Pro: High-quality mode for entire songs and complex audio, maintaining formants during pitch shifts.

41. Explain what kind of controls do each Warp Mode provide in terms of dealing with artifacts.

- Beats Mode: Adjusts Transient Loop Mode to reduce time-stretching artifacts.
- Tones Mode: Provides a Grain Size control to smooth pitch artifacts.
- Texture Mode: Adds Grain Size and Flux controls for granular manipulation.
- Complex/Pro Modes: Optimize CPU load and audio fidelity, especially for vocals and polyphonic textures.

42. What are warp markers and how can they be used to alter the timing of pre-recorded audio? Give an example.

- Warp Markers anchor points in an audio clip that allow for independent time-stretching.
- Example: Move a warp marker on a snare hit to align it with the project's tempo grid.

43. What are Formants?

- Formants are resonant frequencies that define the tonal quality of a sound, independent of pitch. Adjusting formants can change the timbre without affecting pitch, often used in vocal processing.

44. What is the meaning of Grain Size?

- Grain Size refers to the length of individual segments in granular synthesis. Smaller grains produce smoother sounds, while larger grains create choppy, glitch-like effects.

45. How do we set the start point for warping in Ableton?

- In Clip View, drag the Start Marker to the desired position, ensuring the first beat or transient aligns with the grid.

46. What is Flux in Texture Warp Mode?

- Flux adds randomness to grain playback, creating more natural and less mechanical-sounding time-stretching.

47. How can you export a loop in Ableton?

- Select the loop range, go to File > Export Audio/Video, and choose the desired format, bit depth, and sample rate.

48. What is the function of Collect All And Save and Save As Copy?

- Collect All And Save: Gathers all external files used in the project and saves them in the project folder.
- Save As Copy: Saves a copy of the project without collecting external files.

49. How do we export stems in Ableton?

- In the Export Audio/Video window, select All Individual Tracks or manually choose tracks to export as separate stems.

50. What is the purpose of export as loop?

- Ensures that the exported clip loops seamlessly by aligning start and end points, essential for loop-based production and live performances.

51. Explain in detail the controls provided by Beats Warp Mode and how we can use them.

- Preserve Transients: Determines how transients are maintained during time-stretching.
- Transient Loop Modes:

  - Loop Off: Plays each slice once.
  - Loop Forward: Repeats slices forward.
  - Loop Back-and-Forth: Plays slices in reverse and forward loops.

52. What is the Function of Follow and Lead in the clip properties section?

- Follow: Syncs the clip's tempo to the project.
- Lead: Sets the clip as the tempo reference for other clips.

53. What is the role of the Clip Envelope Box?

- Manages clip-based automation for parameters like volume, pitch, and effects within the Clip View.

54. How can we pitch bend audio in Ableton?

- Use the Clip Envelopes to automate pitch changes over time or apply the Transpose knob for static pitch adjustments.

55. How can we add volume envelopes to audio in Ableton?

- Open the Clip Envelope Box, select Volume from the dropdown, and draw the envelope curve to adjust volume dynamically.

56. How can we quantize audio files in Ableton?

- Select the audio clip, press Command + U, and adjust the Quantize Settings to align transients to the grid.

57. What is a Groove Pool and how is it used in Ableton?

- The Groove Pool adds rhythmic and timing variations to clips. Drag grooves from the Groove Library and apply them to audio or MIDI clips for swing and humanization.

58. How can we extract grooves from any audio file in Ableton?

- Right-click an audio clip and choose Extract Groove, adding its timing and rhythm to the Groove Pool for reuse.

59. How can we apply separate grooves to different clips containing the same audio?

- Duplicate the audio clip and apply different grooves from the Groove Pool to each instance, altering their timing independently.

60. How can we commit to a groove? What change will it do?

- Click Commit in the Groove Pool to apply the groove permanently, altering the clip's timing and dynamics.

61. How can we open File Manager in Ableton?

- Go to View > File Manager or click Manage Files in the File Browser.

62. What functionality does Manage Set provide?

- Manage Set allows viewing, relinking, and collecting files used in the project, ensuring no missing files during export or transfer.

63. How can we Manage our Project in the File Manager?

- Use Manage Project to collect, relink, and clean up files, ensuring proper project organization and file integrity.

64. Where can we delete unused project files?

- In Manage Project, select Unused Files and click Delete to remove them from the project folder.

65. What is Packing? How can we create an Ableton Live Pack and what are its benefits?

- Packing compresses a project into a single .alp (Ableton Live Pack) file for easy sharing and backup.
- Create via File > Manage Project > Create Live Pack.

66. What is Collect into Project?

- Gathers all external files into the project folder, ensuring all samples, recordings, and media are stored locally.

67. Where can we search missing files in Ableton?

- In File Manager, click Manage Files > Locate Missing Files to find and relink them.

68. How can we replace samples in a Project?

- Drag a new sample onto an existing clip to replace it or use the Hot-Swap Mode for quick replacement.

69. What is the purpose of hotswapping?

- Hot-Swapping allows for quick replacement of samples, instruments, or effects without navigating through menus, streamlining workflow.

70. Can we freeze audio tracks in Ableton? Explain why it is done.

- Yes, right-click a track and choose Freeze Track to temporarily render it, reducing CPU usage while maintaining editability.

71. Import a drum loop into Ableton Live and add a warp marker on every kick.

- Drag a drum loop into Arrangement View, enable Warp, and double-click each kick transient to add warp markers.

72. How do you set project markers in the arrangement view in live? Save a project with project markers on the bars 1, 16, 32 and 64.

- Right-click the timeline at bars 1, 16, 32, and 64 and choose Add Locator.
- Go to File > Save Live Set to save the project with these markers.

NINE

UNDERSTANDING MIC PLACEMENTS

1. Explain the most used types of Mics to record audio. What are these types based on?

- The most commonly used microphone types are:

  - Dynamic Microphones: Rugged, handle high SPL, ideal for live sound and drums.
  - Condenser Microphones: Sensitive, wide frequency response, suited for studio vocals and acoustic instruments.
  - Ribbon Microphones: Warm, vintage sound, used for guitar amps and strings.

- These types are based on their transducer principle—how they convert sound into electrical signals.

2. Compare a dynamic and condenser Mic in terms of the following:

- Frequency: Dynamic mics have limited frequency range, condensers offer extended highs.
- Diaphragm: Dynamic uses a thicker diaphragm, condenser uses a thin, sensitive diaphragm.
- Internal Circuits: Dynamic mics have simple circuits, condensers need complex preamps and phantom power.
- Durability: Dynamic mics are robust, condensers are delicate.

- Moisture Sensitivity: Condensers are highly sensitive, dynamics are moisture-resistant.
- Feedback: Dynamic mics are less prone to feedback, condensers are more sensitive to it.
- Price: Dynamic mics are generally cheaper, condensers are expensive.
- Sound Pressure Level (SPL): Dynamic mics handle higher SPL, condensers have lower SPL tolerance.

3. What do you understand by frequency response chart?

- A frequency response chart depicts how a microphone responds to different frequencies, showing the mic's sensitivity across the audible spectrum, aiding in choosing the right mic for specific applications.

4. What is feedback? What are the solutions to reducing the chances of getting feedback?

- Feedback occurs when a microphone picks up its own amplified signal, causing a loop.
- Solutions: Use directional mics, lower gain, increase mic-to-speaker distance, and apply EQ filters.

5. Describe what you understand by Microphone frequency response chart.

- It visualizes a mic's output level across frequencies, showing boosts and cuts in specific ranges, crucial for selecting mics for vocals, instruments, or ambient sound.

6. What kind of mics are better suited to record vocals?

- Condenser microphones are preferred for vocals due to their wide frequency response, sensitivity, and accurate sound reproduction.

7. Give examples of an active and a passive mic and also explain what you understand by these terms.

- Active Mic: Neumann U87 (requires phantom power).

- Passive Mic: Shure SM57 (does not require external power).
- Active mics have built-in preamps; passive mics rely on external amplification.

8. Among a condenser mic and a dynamic mic which one has a wider recording field.

- Condenser microphones have a wider recording field due to their sensitivity and broader frequency response.

9. What do you understand by phantom power? How do you activate it in your equipment?

- Phantom power (48V) supplies DC voltage to condenser mics through XLR cables.
- Activate it using the phantom power switch on audio interfaces or mixers.

10. Explain the different diaphragm variations according to the sub-categories of microphone.

- Large-diaphragm condensers: Warm sound, suited for vocals.
- Small-diaphragm condensers: Accurate, for acoustic instruments.
- Dynamic diaphragms: Durable, handle high SPL.

11. What kinds of mic require phantom power?

- Condenser microphones (both large and small diaphragm) need phantom power for their internal preamp and diaphragm charge.
- Active ribbon microphones also require phantom power to operate built-in circuitry.
- Dynamic microphones do not need phantom power as they generate signals through electromagnetic induction.

12. Describe what you understand about the working and uses of the following mics:

- Shotgun Mic: Highly directional with a narrow pickup pattern, used in film, TV production, and field recording to capture sound from a distance while minimizing background noise.
- Boundary Mic: Placed on flat surfaces, it captures reflected sound, making it suitable for conference rooms, theaters, and stage performances.
- USB Mic: Contains built-in audio interfaces, allowing direct connection to computers via USB, commonly used for podcasts, home studios, and voiceovers.

13. What do you understand by the term polar pattern?

- A polar pattern describes a microphone's sensitivity to sound from different directions, determining how it captures sound relative to its position. Common polar patterns include cardioid, omnidirectional, bidirectional, and supercardioid.

14. Describe the various types of polar patterns.

- Cardioid: Heart-shaped pickup, capturing sound from the front while rejecting rear noise, ideal for vocals and podcasts.
- Omnidirectional: Picks up sound equally from all directions, used in ambient recordings and group discussions.
- Bidirectional (Figure-8): Captures sound from the front and back, rejecting the sides, suitable for interviews and stereo recordings.
- Supercardioid/Hypercardioid: Narrower front pickup with slight rear sensitivity, often used in live performances and boom mics.

15. What do you understand by stereo micing? What are the various things that need to be checked while micing in stereo?

- Stereo micing involves using two microphones to capture sound with spatial dimension and depth. Key considerations include:

  - Mic Placement: Ensuring proper angle and distance for accurate stereo imaging.
  - Phase Alignment: Avoiding phase cancellation by maintaining correct polarity.

- ◦ Room Acoustics: Controlling reflections and reverb for a clean stereo field.
- ◦ Mic Type: Choosing suitable mics based on the sound source and environment.

16. Do a comparison between stereo and mono micings.

- Stereo Micing: Uses two mics for a left-right image, creating depth and spatial realism, used in orchestral recordings and ambient sound.
- Mono Micing: Uses a single mic, capturing sound from one point, ideal for vocals, close-miked instruments, and voiceovers, providing a focused and clear signal.

17. What are the different stereo micing techniques and why were they invented in the first place?

- XY Technique: Two cardioid mics at a 90° angle, minimizing phase issues.
- ORTF: Two cardioid mics 17 cm apart at 110°, capturing a wide stereo image with accurate localization.
- NOS: Two cardioid mics 30 cm apart at 90°, offering a natural stereo width.
- Spaced Pair (A/B): Two omnidirectional mics placed apart, providing a wide stereo field but prone to phase issues.
- Mid-Side (M/S): One cardioid mic for the center and one bidirectional mic for the sides, allowing stereo width adjustments in post-production.
- These techniques were developed to accurately capture the spatial qualities of sound, replicating human hearing for immersive audio experiences.

18. Explain briefly about the conditions required for stereo condenser mics to record audio properly.

- Balanced Acoustics: A treated recording space to avoid unwanted reflections.
- Precise Placement: Correct angling and spacing for stereo imaging.
- Stable Phantom Power: Ensuring both mics receive stable 48V power supply.

- Phase Coherence: Ensuring both mics are in phase for accurate stereo reproduction.

19. Explain the following stereo polar patterns:

- XY: Two cardioid mics at 90°, capturing stereo without phase issues.
- ORTF: Two cardioid mics at 110° with 17 cm spacing for realistic stereo width.
- NOS: Two cardioid mics at 90° with 30 cm spacing, balancing width and coherence.
- Spaced: Two mics placed apart, capturing wide stereo but prone to phase shifts.
- Blumlein: Two bidirectional mics at 90°, capturing a natural stereo image with room ambiance.
- M/S: One cardioid for center and one bidirectional for sides, allowing post-production control over stereo width.

20. After recording in M/S recording method, how do we setup the recorded files in Logic to get the desired M/S output?

- Import both recordings into Logic Pro.
- Pan the Mid mic to the center.
- Duplicate the Side mic, pan one hard left and the other hard right.
- Invert the phase of one side mic using Gain Utility.
- Adjust the balance to control stereo width while maintaining the mid-signal integrity.

TEN

RECORDING AND WORKING WITH MIDI IN LOGIC

1. What do you understand by the term MIDI? What does it stand for and when was it standardised?

- MIDI stands for Musical Instrument Digital Interface. It is a communication protocol that allows electronic musical instruments, computers, and other devices to connect and communicate. Introduced in 1983, MIDI was developed by companies like Roland, Sequential Circuits, Yamaha, and others to ensure compatibility between instruments from different manufacturers. MIDI doesn't transmit audio but sends information like note pitch, duration, velocity, and control data.

2. How many Types of MIDI Events are there in Logic?

- In Logic Pro, there are several types of MIDI events, including:
- Note On/Off Events: Trigger and end notes.
- Control Change (CC): Adjust parameters like volume, modulation, or pan.
- Program Change: Switch between instrument patches or sounds.
- Pitch Bend: Gradually changes pitch between notes.
- Aftertouch: Adds expression based on key pressure after a note is played.

- SysEx (System Exclusive): Sends specific data to certain hardware or software instruments.

3. What is a MIDI Note Event and describe it.

- A MIDI Note Event is a command that tells a MIDI device when to play a note, which pitch to play, how loudly (velocity), and for how long. It consists of:
- Note On: Starts the note with velocity information.
- Note Number: Determines pitch (e.g., C3, D4).
- Note Off: Ends the note.
- For example, pressing C4 on a MIDI keyboard sends a MIDI Note On event with a specific velocity, and releasing the key sends a Note Off event.

4. Describe how MIDI information moves from your source to the desired destination.

- MIDI data flows from a MIDI controller (like a keyboard or pad controller) through a MIDI cable or USB connection to a DAW (Logic Pro). Inside the DAW, MIDI information is processed and sent to a software instrument or hardware synthesizer, which then generates sound based on the MIDI data. The DAW can also send MIDI data back to the controller for feedback or synchronization.

5. What are the different types of Software Instruments?

- Synthesizers: Generate sounds through oscillators and filters (e.g., Logic's ES2, Alchemy).
- Samplers: Play back recorded samples (e.g., EXS24, Sampler in Logic).
- Drum Machines: Produce drum sounds through synthesis or samples (e.g., Ultrabeat).
- Virtual Pianos/Organs: Replicate acoustic instruments (e.g., Vintage B3, Electric Piano).
- Orchestral Libraries: Provide realistic strings, brass, woodwinds, and percussion.

6. What do you understand by MIDI CC controls in Logic?

- MIDI CC (Control Change) controls are messages that adjust parameters like volume, pan, modulation, and effects in real-time. In Logic, these controls are mapped to automation lanes in the Piano Roll or Track Automation View. For example, CC1 is usually mapped to modulation wheel, and CC7 controls the volume of a MIDI track.

7. What is a MIDI Controller?

- A MIDI Controller is a hardware device that sends MIDI data to control software instruments and DAWs. It can be a keyboard, pad controller, MIDI guitar, or fader bank, allowing users to trigger notes, adjust parameters, and manipulate sound without generating audio itself.

8. Does a MIDI keyboard make its own sounds?

- No, a MIDI keyboard does not produce its own sounds. It sends MIDI signals to a connected device or DAW, which then generates sound through a software instrument or external hardware.

9. What is the purpose of MIDI Note Numbers? What are the MIDI note numbers of C5, B2, C4?

- MIDI Note Numbers represent specific pitches. The numbering starts from C-1 (0) to G9 (127).

  - C5: MIDI note number 72.
  - B2: MIDI note number 47.
  - C4: MIDI note number 60 (also known as Middle C).

10. Where can we find the available MIDI CC controls for your instrument in Logic?

- In Logic Pro, MIDI CC controls are found in the Piano Roll's Automation View and the MIDI Environment. You can also access them through the Smart Controls Panel when a software instrument is loaded, where various CC parameters are assigned for modulation, pitch bend, and more.

11. Explain if the following controls are CC controls or Note Event controls:

- Modwheel: CC control (typically CC1 for modulation).
- Fader Knob: CC control (commonly CC7 for volume).
- Pads: Note Event control (triggering MIDI notes).
- Drum Pads: Note Event control (sending MIDI note data for drum hits).

12. What are the various types of MIDI information that we can view in Logic's LCD?

- In Logic's Transport LCD, you can view:
- MIDI In/Out Indicators: Show incoming and outgoing MIDI data.
- Note Data: Displays the MIDI note being played.
- Velocity: Shows the intensity of a played note.
- Channel Information: Displays the active MIDI channel.
- Time Position: Shows the position of MIDI events in bars, beats, and ticks.

13. What are MIDI Channels and how many MIDI channels are there in Logic?

- A MIDI Channel is an independent path for MIDI data, allowing multiple instruments to be controlled simultaneously. There are 16 MIDI channels in Logic, each capable of handling separate MIDI data streams within a single MIDI cable or track.

14. Does Velocity control Volume?

- Yes, MIDI velocity controls the volume or intensity of a note. Higher velocity values produce louder sounds, while lower values produce softer sounds, adding dynamic expression to MIDI performances.

15. Does the Modwheel of your MIDI controller always control vibrato?

- No, the Modwheel (CC1) is typically assigned to vibrato by default, but it can be mapped to control various parameters like filter cutoff, pitch bend, or effect depth depending on the software instrument.

16. How many types of MIDI Controllers are used for working with MIDI? Describe a few examples.

- Keyboard Controllers: (e.g., AKAI MPK, Novation Launchkey) – Trigger notes and control software instruments.
- Pad Controllers: (e.g., Ableton Push, Akai MPD) – Used for drums, loops, and samples.
- Fader/Knob Controllers: (e.g., Korg NanoKontrol) – Adjust volumes, pans, and automation parameters.
- MIDI Guitar Controllers: (e.g., Jamstik) – Play MIDI instruments using a guitar interface.

17. What are weighted and non-weighted keys on a MIDI Controller?

- Weighted Keys: Mimic the feel of acoustic piano keys with resistance, preferred by pianists for realistic performance.
- Non-weighted Keys: Light and responsive, suitable for synth playing and fast MIDI input.

18. How do you record a MIDI region for 4 bars, then stretch it to half-time using the resize pointer?

- Record the MIDI region by pressing R and playing for 4 bars.
- Select the region, grab the Resize Pointer Tool, hold Option, and drag the edge to stretch it, effectively doubling its length to 8 bars and playing at half-time.

19. How to record MIDI in Logic?

- Setup: Create a new Software Instrument Track.
- Arm Recording: Click the R button on the track.
- Record: Press R on the keyboard and play on your MIDI controller.
- Stop Recording: Press the Spacebar.
- The recorded MIDI region appears in the timeline, ready for editing.

20. Describe two ways by which we can bring all the notes in a MIDI region to the same velocity.

- Velocity Tool: Select all notes, use the Velocity Tool in the Piano Roll, and drag to the desired velocity.
- MIDI Transform Function: Open Functions > MIDI Transform > Fixed Velocity, set the target velocity, and apply it to all selected notes.

21. Describe how you fix the note lengths of all the MIDI note events in Logic.

- To fix note lengths for all MIDI notes:
- Open the Piano Roll.
- Select all notes using Command + A.
- Click the Time Quantize dropdown in the Piano Roll inspector and choose a note length (e.g., 1/8 or 1/16).
- Alternatively, use Functions > MIDI Transform > Fixed Note Length to apply a uniform length to all selected notes.

22. How can you configure a MIDI region in a way that its colours are the same as that of the region?

- In the Tracks Area, select the MIDI region.
- Open the Region Inspector on the left.
- Click the Color dropdown and select Same as Track Color to ensure that the region inherits the track's color, making it visually consistent and easy to manage.

23. What is the shortcut for shifting MIDI notes by Semitones and Octaves in a MIDI region in Logic?

- Shift by Semitone: Select notes and press Option + Up/Down Arrow.
- Shift by Octave: Press Shift + Option + Up/Down Arrow.

24. How can we copy MIDI notes in Logic?

- Select the desired notes in the Piano Roll.
- Hold Option and drag the notes to a new position to create a copy.
- Alternatively, use Command + C (copy) and Command + V (paste) to duplicate MIDI notes within the region.

25. Explain a few methods of selecting a note in Logic.

- Single Click: Click on an individual note in the Piano Roll.
- Marquee Tool: Drag the marquee selection box around multiple notes.
- Shift + Click: Add or remove individual notes from a selection.
- Select All: Use Command + A to select all notes in the region.

26. Explain a few methods for deleting notes in Logic.

- Select the note and press Delete.
- Use the Eraser Tool in the Piano Roll.
- Marquee-select multiple notes and press Delete.
- Use MIDI Transform with the Delete Range option for precise deletions.

27. What do you understand by capture recording and what is its shortcut in Logic?

- Capture Recording allows recording MIDI retroactively even if you didn't press record. Logic continuously listens to MIDI input and lets you retrieve what you played.

  - Shortcut: Press Shift + R to capture the last played MIDI performance into the selected track.

28. How can we duplicate regions and MIDI notes multiple times in Logic?

- Duplicate Regions: Select the region, press Command + D to duplicate it sequentially.
- Duplicate MIDI Notes: In the Piano Roll, select notes, hold Option + Shift, and drag to create multiple duplicates in one move.

29. Is it possible while working with MIDI in Logic to:

- Create Take Folders: Yes, by recording MIDI over existing regions with Cycle Mode enabled, Logic automatically creates take folders for comping.

- Punch In/Out: Yes, enable Punch In/Out in the transport bar, set the punch range, and start recording. Logic will only record between the punch-in and punch-out points.
- These features are beneficial as they allow multiple takes for detailed editing and precise recording for complex MIDI performances.

30. Explain the replace mode in Logic.

- Replace Mode allows you to overwrite existing MIDI data during recording:

  - Activate Replace in the transport bar.
  - Play new MIDI input, and Logic will replace the existing MIDI notes in the region rather than merging them.

- This is beneficial for correcting specific sections without manual deletion but can be a drawback if you need to keep previous takes.

31. What do you understand by the terms MIDI-In and MIDI-Out?

- MIDI-In: Refers to the incoming MIDI data from an external controller or device into Logic.
- MIDI-Out: Refers to MIDI data sent from Logic to external instruments, controllers, or other DAWs.

32. Explain all the ways you can change CC controls in Logic.

- Piano Roll Automation Lane: Add and adjust CC data like modulation, expression, or pitch bend.
- Smart Controls: Use knobs and sliders to modify assigned CC parameters.
- MIDI Draw in the Tracks Area: Automate CC changes directly on the MIDI region.
- MIDI Event List Editor: Edit CC values numerically for precise control.

33. What is the MIDI Event List in Logic?

- The MIDI Event List is a detailed editor displaying all MIDI data in a track, including note events, velocities, CC messages, pitch bends, and more. It allows manual editing of each event's parameters such as start time, length, and value.

34. Explain all the ways of detecting CC controls in Logic.

- MIDI Monitor in the Environment Window: Displays real-time incoming MIDI data.
- Piano Roll Automation Lane: Shows active CC data for selected regions.
- MIDI Input Display in the Transport Bar: Shows current MIDI messages received by Logic.
- MIDI Event List: Displays all CC events recorded or drawn in the MIDI region.

35. Where can we edit CC events in Logic?

- Piano Roll Editor: Adjust and draw CC automation.
- Track Automation View: Edit CC data on the main timeline.
- MIDI Event List Editor: Change CC values precisely by editing event parameters.

36. How can you copy MIDI events in Logic? Explain how you can add curves to MIDI CC automations.

- Copy MIDI Events: Select the MIDI events in the Piano Roll, hold Option, and drag them to the desired location.
- Add Curves to MIDI CC Automation:

  - Open the Piano Roll Automation Lane.
  - Draw a straight line, then use the Automation Curve Tool (hold Control + Shift while dragging the line) to create smooth curves for expressive changes in parameters like modulation, volume, or pitch bend.

37. What is the function of the catch button in Logic?

- The Catch button ensures that the playhead remains in view during playback or recording. When enabled, Logic automatically scrolls the timeline as the playhead moves, keeping your current playback position visible without manual scrolling.

38. Explain how you can create harmonies by using scale quantisation in Logic.

- Scale Quantisation snaps MIDI notes to a selected musical scale. To create harmonies:

  - Open the Piano Roll and select all notes.
  - In the Scale Quantise dropdown, choose a scale (e.g., C Major).
  - Duplicate the melody on a new track, then shift notes by intervals (like thirds or fifths).
  - Apply Scale Quantisation to ensure all harmonised notes fit the key.

39. What is the collapse mode and what are the benefits of using this mode?

- Collapse Mode in the Piano Roll hides all unused MIDI note rows, showing only notes that exist in the selected region.

  - Benefits: Reduces visual clutter, making it easier to edit patterns, especially in drum programming, as only active drum hits are visible.

40. Describe in detail what you fully understand by quantisation.

- Quantisation aligns MIDI notes to a chosen grid (e.g., 1/8, 1/16) to correct timing errors.

  - Types:

    - Hard Quantisation: Snaps notes exactly to the grid.
    - Soft Quantisation (Q-Strength): Moves notes closer to the grid while retaining some human feel.
    - Swing Quantisation: Shifts alternate notes to create a groove.

  - Used to refine performances while maintaining musicality.

41. How do you force Legato in Logic?

- Select MIDI notes in the Piano Roll.
- Press Shift + L to extend each note until it meets the next, ensuring seamless note transitions, especially for sustaining instruments like strings or pads.

42. What do you understand by the term Force Legato and its keyboard shortcut?

- Force Legato ensures that selected notes extend to the start of the next note.

  - Shortcut: Shift + L.

43. What are the functions of the List editor in Logic?

- The List Editor displays all MIDI events (notes, CC data, pitch bends) in a numerical list.

  - Functions:

    - Edit note timings, velocities, and lengths with precision.
    - View and modify all MIDI events without graphical interface distractions.
    - Delete, duplicate, or adjust MIDI events easily.

44. What are the purposes of the Time Handle and demonstrate some of its uses.

- The Time Handle allows you to select and manipulate a specific time range in the Piano Roll.

  - Uses:

    - Stretching MIDI patterns to slow down or speed up note sequences.
    - Moving entire sections of MIDI data to new positions in the timeline.

45. What is the function of "define brush pattern"?

- Define Brush Pattern in Logic lets you create custom MIDI note patterns that can be drawn using the Brush Tool.

  - Example: Design a drum fill pattern and apply it repeatedly by clicking and dragging in the Piano Roll.

46. What is the function of the Step Editor and the Score Editor?

- Step Editor: Provides a grid-based view for precise editing of MIDI data like velocity, pitch bend, and modulation on a per-step basis.
- Score Editor: Displays MIDI data as traditional musical notation, allowing for editing and printing sheet music.

47. What are the meanings of the following:

- Q Strength: Adjusts how tightly notes snap to the grid after quantisation.
- Q Range: Determines which notes are affected by quantisation based on their distance from the grid.
- Q Flam: Offsets selected notes slightly from each other to create a "flam" effect, common in drum rolls.

48. Explain the different ways quantisation can be done in Logic. Explain the difference between event base quantisation and region-based quantisation.

- Region-Based Quantisation: Applies quantisation to an entire region, affecting all contained notes.
- Event-Based Quantisation: Applies quantisation to individually selected notes or events.
- Region quantisation is quick for entire performances, while event quantisation allows for precise edits on specific notes.

49. How can we freeze a track in Logic and what are its uses?

- Right-click a track and choose Freeze Track.

- Logic renders the track as audio, reducing CPU usage while retaining the ability to unfreeze for later edits.

50. What is the function of replace mode in Logic and what are its uses?

- Replace Mode overwrites existing MIDI data during recording, ideal for correcting parts of a performance without manually deleting old notes.

51. How can you export MIDI out of Logic?

- Select the MIDI region, go to File > Export > Selection as MIDI File, and save the .MID file for use in other DAWs or hardware instruments.

52. How do you create notes in the Piano Roll Editor?

- Use the Pencil Tool to click on the desired pitch and time grid position, creating a new note. Drag to adjust length.

53. How do you adjust note lengths in the Piano Roll Editor?

- Select notes and drag their ends to lengthen or shorten them. Use Shift + Drag for fine adjustments.

54. How do you adjust the velocity of the notes in the Piano Roll Editor?

- Select a note and drag the Velocity Handle below it or use the Velocity Tool to change the intensity of multiple notes simultaneously.

55. In the Piano Roll Editor, how do you view only those lanes occupied by MIDI Notes?

- Enable Collapse Mode by clicking the Collapse icon, showing only active note lanes.

56. How do you quickly paint multiple notes of the same length?

- Use the Brush Tool and hold Shift to paint consecutive notes with uniform length.

57. How do you create a crescendo using note velocities?

- Select a series of notes, open the Velocity Lane, and use the Line Tool to draw a gradual increase in velocity from the first to the last note.

58. How do you create MIDI Control Data?

- Open the Automation Lane in the Piano Roll, select a CC parameter (e.g., Modulation), and use the Pencil Tool to draw automation data.

59. How do you curve lines in MIDI Automation?

- After drawing a line, hold Control + Shift and drag the line to create a curve, allowing smooth dynamic changes.

60. How do you copy a section of automation in MIDI Draw?

- Select the automation section with the Marquee Tool, press Command + C, move the playhead, and press Command + V to paste.

61. How can you check the pitch and velocity of a note in the Piano Roll?

- Hover over a note to display its pitch and velocity in the Info Bar at the top of the Piano Roll.

62. How do you merge a new recording to an existing MIDI region?

- Enable Overlapping Recordings Merge in Preferences > Recording or manually select both regions and press Command + J to join them.

63. How can you time-correct a MIDI region?

- Select the region and apply Quantisation in the Region Inspector or use Flex Time for non-linear adjustments.

64. How do you choose default region parameters for new MIDI recording?

- Go to Preferences > Recording > MIDI, set default quantisation, velocity, and MIDI channel settings for all new recordings.

65. How do you automatically arpeggiate chords in Ableton?

- Load the Arpeggiator MIDI Effect on a MIDI track, adjust the Rate, Style, and Octave Range to generate arpeggios automatically when chords are played.

66. What keyboard shortcut can you use in Logic to make the recorded MIDI note events not overlap on each other?

- The shortcut is Shift + Backslash (\), which applies Force Legato.
- This extends each selected note until the beginning of the next note, ensuring no overlapping MIDI events, crucial for maintaining clarity and precision in MIDI sequences, especially for instruments like piano or strings.

67. How do you choose default region parameters for new MIDI recording?

- To set default region parameters for all new MIDI recordings in Logic:

  - Go to Logic Pro > Preferences > Recording.
  - In the MIDI section, you can set:

    - Quantisation settings (e.g., 1/16 notes for automatic timing correction).
    - Default velocity for new notes.
    - Record MIDI to separate tracks or merge onto one.
    - Auto-demix by channel if multitrack recording is needed.

- This ensures consistency across all MIDI regions recorded during a session, saving time and maintaining workflow efficiency.

68. How do you automatically arpeggiate chords in Ableton?

- In Ableton Live, arpeggiating chords automatically involves:

- Dragging the Arpeggiator MIDI Effect onto your MIDI track.
- Adjusting the Rate (speed of arpeggiation), Style (up, down, up-down, random), and Octave Range to define how many octaves the arpeggio covers.
- Use the Gate control to adjust the note length and the Steps parameter to determine the sequence length.
- When you play a chord on your MIDI controller, Ableton will trigger individual notes in succession, creating an arpeggio without manual MIDI editing.

ELEVEN

PROGRAMMING MIDI IN ABLETON

1. How do we add MIDI tracks?

- In Ableton Live, you can add a MIDI track by:

  - Pressing Command + Shift + T (Mac) or Ctrl + Shift + T (Windows).
  - Alternatively, right-click in the Track Area and select Insert MIDI Track.

- This creates a track designed for MIDI instruments and clips.

2. How can we load software instruments in a MIDI track?

- Drag a software instrument (e.g., Analog, Operator, or Simpler) from the Browser into a MIDI track.
- Instruments can also be loaded by double-clicking an instrument from the Instruments Section in the Browser when a MIDI track is selected.
- This enables MIDI data on the track to trigger sounds from the software instrument.

3. How can we record MIDI in Ableton?

- Arm the MIDI track by clicking the Record Arm button (red circle) on the track.

- Press Session Record (F9) or click the main Record button in the transport bar.
- Play your MIDI controller, and the MIDI notes are recorded into the clip slot or arrangement view depending on the selected mode.

4. How can we add a blank MIDI clip?

- Double-click on an empty slot in the Session View of a MIDI track.
- Alternatively, in Arrangement View, highlight a section, right-click, and select Insert MIDI Clip.
- This creates a blank clip ready for note input.

5. How can we draw MIDI notes in Ableton?

- Enter the MIDI Editor by double-clicking a MIDI clip.
- Use the Pencil Tool (activated by pressing B) to draw MIDI notes on the grid.
- Click to place a note, and drag to adjust its length.

6. What is the shortcut for the Pencil Tool?

- The shortcut is B.
- Pressing B toggles the Pencil Tool on and off, allowing you to switch quickly between drawing and selecting MIDI notes.

7. What are the two ways in which we can resize MIDI notes?

- Drag the Note Edge: Select the MIDI note and drag its edge to adjust its length.
- Shortcut Method: Select the note, hold Shift + Arrow Keys to increase or decrease note length precisely.

8. How can we copy or duplicate notes in Ableton?

- Select the MIDI notes, press Command + C (Mac) or Ctrl + C (Windows) to copy, and Command + V (Mac) or Ctrl + V (Windows) to paste.
- Use Command + D (Mac) or Ctrl + D (Windows) to quickly duplicate selected notes in succession.

9. What is Velocity and how do we control it in Ableton?

- Velocity determines how hard a note is played, affecting volume and timbre.
- In the MIDI Editor, adjust velocity by dragging the velocity markers under each note.
- Use the Velocity MIDI Effect to set and modify velocity ranges and sensitivity dynamically.

10. How can we change pitch of MIDI in octaves and semitones?

- Semitones: Select notes and press Arrow Up/Down.
- Octaves: Press Shift + Arrow Up/Down to move notes by octaves.

11. What is Chance and how can we use it in Ableton?

- Chance determines the probability of a MIDI note being played.

  - In the MIDI Editor, enable the Chance Editor Lane and adjust the Chance value (0% to 100%) for each note.

- This creates dynamic and evolving sequences by introducing randomness.

12. What is the role of Velocity Range in Ableton?

- The Velocity Range sets a minimum and maximum velocity for MIDI notes, adding dynamic variation.

  - Use the Velocity MIDI Effect to define a range, ensuring notes are played with varying intensity even when the original velocity is constant.

13. How can we randomize velocity and chance in Ableton?

- Use the Velocity MIDI Effect with the Random parameter to randomize note velocities within a defined range.

- Adjust Chance values in the MIDI Editor to randomly skip or trigger notes during playback.

14. How can we delete notes from MIDI clips?

- Select the MIDI notes and press Delete.
- Alternatively, use the Eraser Tool by holding Command (Mac) or Ctrl (Windows) and clicking on notes.

15. How can we select multiple notes within a MIDI clip?

- Drag to Select: Click and drag over multiple notes.
- Shift + Click: Select individual notes while holding Shift.
- Command + A (Mac) or Ctrl + A (Windows) selects all notes in the clip.

16. What is Capture recording? How does it work and how can it benefit us?

- Capture Recording records MIDI input even when you haven't pressed record.
- Press Capture (icon next to the transport bar) after playing.
- Ableton retrieves the last played MIDI data and creates a clip.
- This is beneficial for spontaneous performances and ideas that you didn't initially record but want to preserve.

17. How can we record MIDI while making take folders?

- Enable Loop Recording in Arrangement View.
- Each loop pass creates a take in the Take Lane, allowing you to choose or comp the best segments later, ensuring flexible and detailed MIDI editing.

18. Can we comp MIDI in Ableton?

- Yes, comping MIDI is possible by using the Take Lanes in Arrangement View, similar to audio comping, allowing seamless editing and combining of different takes into a perfect performance.

19. How can we do Punch In and Punch Out while recording MIDI?

- Enable Punch In/Out in the transport bar by setting the punch range using the loop braces.
- Recording starts automatically at the punch-in point and stops at the punch-out point, ensuring precise recording in defined sections.

20. How do we Quantize MIDI in Ableton? How can we access Quantization setting within Ableton?

- Select MIDI notes and press Command + U (Mac) or Ctrl + U (Windows) to quantize.
- Access settings through Edit > Quantize Settings, adjusting parameters like grid size, quantize amount, and swing for precise or groove-based quantisation.

21. What is the purpose of Record Quantization?

- Record Quantization automatically aligns MIDI notes to a selected grid as they are recorded. This ensures that notes are rhythmically precise without manual quantization after recording, making it ideal for fast-paced workflows and live performances.

22. What is Step Input Method and how do we do it in Ableton?

- The Step Input Method allows users to enter MIDI notes one step at a time without continuous playing:

  ○ Open the MIDI Editor.
  ○ Enable Computer MIDI Keyboard (M).
  ○ Use the arrow keys to navigate the grid and enter notes step by step, useful for programming complex sequences with precision.

23. What are the uses of MIDI Editor Preview button?

- The MIDI Editor Preview button allows real-time audio preview of selected MIDI notes during editing, ensuring immediate auditory feedback, which is essential for fine-tuning sequences and harmonies.

24. What is the function of the Fold button and how do we use it?

- The Fold button in the MIDI Editor hides all rows without MIDI notes, showing only active lanes. This is particularly useful in drum programming, focusing solely on triggered samples for efficient editing.

25. How do we fold MIDI clips according to scales in Ableton?

- In the MIDI Editor, select a scale from the Scale dropdown.
- Enable Fold to display only the notes within the selected scale, ensuring all MIDI inputs remain in key, aiding in harmonic consistency.

26. What are Time Handles?

- Time Handles are tools used to stretch or compress MIDI sequences within the MIDI Editor, allowing tempo manipulation within a specific range for creative timing effects or correction.

27. How can we double or halve the size of MIDI notes?

- Double size: Select notes and press Shift + Command + Right Arrow (Mac) or Shift + Ctrl + Right Arrow (Windows).
- Halve size: Use Shift + Command + Left Arrow (Mac) or Shift + Ctrl + Left Arrow (Windows).

28. What is Legato and what does it do in Ableton?

- Legato extends each MIDI note to the start of the next, creating smooth, connected phrases, especially for instruments like strings, pads, and synth leads.

29. How do we duplicate MIDI loops?

- Select the MIDI loop and press Command + D (Mac) or Ctrl + D (Windows) to duplicate it instantly within the timeline.

30. How can we draw CC controls?

- Open the MIDI Clip View, select Envelopes, choose the desired CC parameter, and use the Pencil Tool (B) to draw automation curves for dynamic modulation and control.

31. How can we add curves to CC control envelopes?

- After drawing a straight automation line, hold Alt (Mac) or Ctrl (Windows) and drag the line to create smooth curves, adding natural modulation to parameters like filter cutoff or pitch bend.

32. How can we use Pitch Bend and Modulation for particular notes within a MIDI clip?

- Select the note, open the Envelope Editor, choose Pitch Bend or Modulation from the dropdown, and draw automation specific to that note, enabling expressive pitch slides or dynamic modulation.

33. How can we do MIDI mappings in Ableton?

- Enter MIDI Map Mode (Command + M), click on any parameter in Ableton, and then press a key or move a knob on your MIDI controller to assign it. Exit MIDI Map Mode to save assignments.

34. How can we Invert the Range of MIDI parameters mapped to external MIDI controls?

- In MIDI Map Mode, select the mapped parameter in the MIDI Mapping Browser, adjust the Min and Max values, and invert the range by swapping these values, causing higher controller values to produce lower parameter outputs and vice versa.

35. How do we setup a MIDI keyboard controller with Ableton?

- Go to Preferences > Link/MIDI, enable your MIDI controller in the Input and Output sections, and ensure Track, Sync, and Remote options are correctly activated for proper communication.

36. How can we record the movements of external MIDI controllers into Ableton?

- Arm the track for recording, manipulate your MIDI controller's knobs or faders during playback, and Ableton records these movements as MIDI automation for real-time modulation.

37. Explain MPE.

- MPE (MIDI Polyphonic Expression) extends MIDI's capabilities, allowing each note to have independent pitch bend, modulation, and pressure data, enhancing expressiveness in instruments like ROLI Seaboard.

38. How can we use MPE functionality in Ableton?

- Load an MPE-compatible instrument (like Wavetable), enable MPE Mode, and use an MPE controller to apply unique modulations per note, such as pitch slides or dynamic filter adjustments.

39. What is the purpose of Pressure and Slide in the MPE section of a MIDI clip?

- Pressure controls the intensity applied to each note, affecting parameters like volume or cutoff.
- Slide allows pitch glides or parameter modulations across the key surface, providing continuous control over timbre and pitch.

40. Which instruments in Ableton support MPE?

- Instruments like Wavetable, Simpler, Sampler, and Operator support MPE, allowing advanced modulation and expression per note.

41. How can we use our computer keyboard as a MIDI keyboard? What are its drawbacks?

- Enable Computer MIDI Keyboard (M) to use your computer keys as a MIDI input device.

- Drawbacks: Limited range, lack of velocity sensitivity, and fewer keys compared to a dedicated MIDI controller.

42. What is the function of the MIDI overdub button?

- The MIDI Overdub button allows adding new notes or automation to an existing MIDI clip during playback without erasing previous recordings, perfect for layering parts incrementally.

43. How do we turn on Automation Arm?

- Click the Automation Arm button (circle icon) in the top bar, allowing Ableton to record automation during playback or recording.

44. How do we export MIDI files from Ableton?

- Select the MIDI clip, right-click, and choose Export MIDI Clip or use File > Export MIDI Clip to save the sequence as a .MID file.

45. How can we create a crescendo using note velocities in Ableton?

- In the Velocity Editor, select notes, and use the Draw Tool (B) with a linear gradient to gradually increase velocities, creating a dynamic crescendo effect.

46. How can we merge two MIDI clips together?

- Select both MIDI clips, right-click, and choose Consolidate (Command + J), merging them into a single editable MIDI clip.

47. How can we extract grooves from MIDI clips in Ableton?

- Right-click on a MIDI clip and select Extract Groove. The groove is added to the Groove Pool, where it can be applied to other clips for rhythm and feel consistency.

48. How can we convert audio to MIDI in Ableton? Explain the 3 algorithms in Ableton with examples.

- In Ableton Live, audio can be converted to MIDI through three algorithms:

  - Convert Harmony to MIDI: Extracts chord progressions from harmonic audio (e.g., piano chords), turning them into playable MIDI.
  - Convert Melody to MIDI: Captures monophonic melodies (e.g., a vocal line) and translates them to MIDI.
  - Convert Drums to MIDI: Detects percussive hits from a drum loop and maps them to MIDI drum pads, ideal for layering and sound replacement.

- Example: Convert a bassline from an audio track to MIDI using Convert Melody to MIDI, then modify or replace it with a synthesised bass instrument.

49. How can we slice a sample or loop using MIDI?

- Right-click an audio loop and select Slice to New MIDI Track.
- Choose a slicing preset (e.g., slice by beat, transient, or warp markers).
- Ableton creates a Drum Rack with each slice mapped to a MIDI pad for triggering and rearranging, perfect for chopping and remixing samples.

50. Create a MIDI clip, add a few different notes. Now duplicate the loop from the clip overview section. After that select all the notes in the MIDI clip and inverse them.

- Steps:

  - Create MIDI Clip: Double-click an empty slot, add notes using the Pencil Tool (B).
  - Duplicate Loop: Click the loop bracket in the clip overview and drag to extend.
  - Select All Notes: Press Command + A (Mac) or Ctrl + A (Windows).
  - Invert Notes: Right-click and select Invert, flipping the pitch order for creative variations.

51. Record a MIDI clip of two bars using your laptop as a MIDI keyboard, then quantise the note events that aren't locked in with the grid.

- Steps:

    - Enable Computer MIDI Keyboard (M).
    - Press Record (F9) and play notes using the laptop keyboard.
    - Select the recorded clip, press Command + U (Mac) or Ctrl + U (Windows) to quantise, aligning offbeat notes to the grid.

52. How can you minimise CPU usage when working with multiple MIDI Tracks?

- Freeze MIDI tracks by right-clicking and selecting Freeze Track.
- Use Track Grouping to process multiple tracks with shared effects.
- Bounce MIDI to Audio for CPU-heavy instruments by exporting or resampling the track.

53. How can view and edit multiple MIDI clips in Ableton Live at the same time?

- Enable Multi-Clip Editing by selecting multiple MIDI clips (Shift + Click), then double-click to open them in the MIDI Editor simultaneously, allowing cross-clip editing for harmonisation or rhythmic alignment.

54. Show from where in Ableton you can select the channel MIDI input.

- In the Track I/O section, click the dropdown under MIDI From to select the MIDI input source (e.g., external controller, another MIDI track, or virtual instruments).

55. Record a hi-hat pattern using Ableton's Drum Rack and then extract the groove from that pattern. Save the groove in your browser and use it on a 2-bar MIDI drum loop of your choice.

- Steps:

    - Load Drum Rack and record a hi-hat pattern.
    - Right-click the clip and select Extract Groove.
    - Save the extracted groove in the Groove Pool.

- ○ Apply it to any 2-bar drum loop by dragging the groove from the pool onto the loop clip.

56. Program a 1-bar MIDI drum loop, duplicate it, and then apply two different grooves in each clip.

- Steps:

  - ○ Create a 1-bar drum loop in the MIDI Editor.
  - ○ Duplicate it using Command + D.
  - ○ Open the Groove Pool and apply one groove to the first clip and a different groove to the second for rhythmic variation.

57. Take a 2-bar audio loop and slice it to a new MIDI track. Then rearrange your previous sample into something different from the original sample.

- Steps:

  - ○ Right-click the 2-bar loop and choose Slice to New MIDI Track.
  - ○ In the Drum Rack, rearrange slices by triggering them in different orders.
  - ○ Add effects or pitch changes to individual slices for creative manipulation.

TWELVE

USING DRUMMER TRACKS IN LOGIC

1. How can you create Drummer tracks in Logic?

- In Logic Pro, go to Track > New Drummer Track or click the + icon and select Drummer from the track type options.
- Choose a drummer style (e.g., Rock, Electronic, Hip Hop) and Logic automatically generates a drum pattern that can be customized in the Drummer Editor.

2. What is the purpose of XY pad in Drummer?

- The XY Pad in the Drummer Editor controls the complexity and loudness of the drum pattern.
- Moving the circle horizontally adjusts complexity (left for simple, right for complex), and vertically adjusts loudness (up for louder, down for quieter).
- This allows quick, intuitive adjustments to the drum groove.

3. How can you save drummer presets in Logic?

- Customize your drum pattern in the Drummer Editor.
- Click the Save button at the top of the editor or go to Settings > Save as Default.
- Name the preset, and it will be available in the Library under the User Presets section for future use.

4. What is the function of Follow in Drummer?

- The Follow function makes the drummer track follow the rhythm of another track, such as bass or guitar.
- Enable it in the Drummer Editor by selecting a track from the Follow dropdown.
- This ensures the drum pattern complements the timing and groove of the chosen instrument track.

5. How to control and add fills in Drummer?

- Use the Fills knob in the Drummer Editor to adjust the frequency and intensity of drum fills.
- Turn the knob right for more frequent and complex fills, left for fewer and simpler fills.
- Add manual fills by splitting the drummer region and editing specific segments.

6. How can you select multi-outputs in Drummer and what are its benefits?

- Create a drummer track, then go to Track > Configure Track Header and enable Multi-Output.
- Benefits include assigning each drum component (kick, snare, hi-hat) to individual mixer channels, allowing separate EQ, compression, and effects for each drum element.

7. How can you convert a Drum Region to a MIDI Region?

- Right-click the drummer region and select Convert to MIDI Region.
- This converts the automated drummer pattern into editable MIDI notes, providing full control over individual drum hits.

8. How can you add 8th/16th note swing in Drummer?

- In the Drummer Editor, adjust the Swing slider under the Feel section.
- Choose 8th or 16th notes, then move the slider right for more swing (laid-back feel) or left for a straighter rhythm.

9. What is the purpose of the following: i) Feel, ii) Pull, iii) Push

- Feel: Adjusts the drummer's timing between humanized loose and tight precision.
- Pull: Pulls the drummer slightly behind the beat for a relaxed feel.
- Push: Pushes the drummer slightly ahead of the beat, adding energy and urgency to the rhythm.

10. What are ghost notes and how can you add or delete ghost notes in Logic?

- Ghost notes are soft, subtle drum hits (usually on the snare) that add groove without overpowering the main rhythm.
- After converting to MIDI, add ghost notes by manually placing low-velocity hits on offbeats. Delete by selecting and pressing Delete.

11. How can you customize your HiHats in the Drummer Tracks?

- In the Drummer Editor, use the Hi-Hat knob to adjust openness.
- Convert to MIDI and manually adjust note lengths, velocities, and swing for precise hi-hat patterns.

12. When we take a new drummer track, we get 8 bars of content, how can we add to those bars and make variations in the new bars?

- Extend the drummer region by dragging its edge.
- Use the Editor's Variation controls to create new patterns in the added bars, ensuring variation while maintaining groove.

13. How do you open the Drum Library in Logic?

- Select a drummer track and click the Library button (folder icon) or press Y to open the drum library, where you can browse and load different drummer kits and styles.

14. How to Change Drum Kits in Drummer?

- Open the Library (Y) and select a new kit from available categories like Rock, Electronic, or Percussion.
- Changing kits retains the pattern but replaces the drum sounds, allowing easy sound experimentation.

15. Is it possible in Drummer to adjust the gain of each drum part individually?

- Yes, by enabling Multi-Output, then adjusting the gain of each drum component separately in the mixer using the individual output channels.

16. Is it possible in Drummer to change the gain of percussion? If yes, then how.

- After enabling Multi-Output, select the Percussion channel in the mixer and adjust its gain slider or insert a Gain plugin for precise control.

17. How can you tweak and make variations of the kick, snare, hi-hat, and percussion in Drummer Tracks in Logic?

- Convert the drummer region to MIDI, then manually adjust note placements, velocities, and add effects.
- Use the Step Sequencer or Piano Roll for intricate variations.

18. How can you solo a particular section of the drummer track in Logic?

- Use the Solo button (S) on the track header or solo individual drum components in the mixer when using Multi-Output mode.

19. How can you access the Drummer Editor in Logic?

- Double-click on the drummer track region or select the track and press E to open the Drummer Editor at the bottom of the screen.

20. How can you change the drummer in a drummer track but the pattern and settings don't change?

- In the Drummer Editor, select a different drummer from the Drummer menu while keeping the current pattern and settings intact.

21. How can we change Drumkits but not change the drummer in Logic?

- In the Library (Y), select a different drum kit while keeping the same drummer in the Drummer Editor, allowing sound changes without altering the rhythm.

22. How do you mute/unmute drum parts?

- Open the Drummer Editor or convert the drummer track to MIDI.
- In the Drummer Editor, click on individual drum elements to toggle their presence (e.g., clicking the kick icon mutes/unmutes it).
- After converting to MIDI, mute/unmute specific drum parts by selecting their regions in the Piano Roll and pressing M or by muting channels in the Mixer when using Multi-Output Mode.

23. How do you make the drummer play softer or louder, simpler or more complex?

- Use the XY Pad in the Drummer Editor:

  - Move the pad vertically for softer (down) or louder (up) drums.
  - Move it horizontally for a simpler (left) or more complex (right) rhythm.

- Adjust the Feel knob for timing variations and the Fills knob for fill complexity and intensity.

24. How do you access the feel knob and make the drummer play behind or ahead of the beat?

- Open the Drummer Editor by double-clicking the drummer region.
- Adjust the Feel knob:

  - Turn it left to make the drummer play slightly behind the beat (laid-back feel).

- ◦ Turn it right to make the drummer play slightly ahead of the beat (urgent, energetic feel).

25. When you customise a drum kit, how can you access the available drum kit pieces?

- In the Drummer Editor, click the Drum Kit icon at the bottom right to open the Drum Kit Designer.
- This shows all available pieces of the selected drum kit (kick, snare, hi-hats, cymbals, toms).
- Swap pieces by clicking individual drums and selecting alternatives from the Library, allowing you to mix and match kit components.

26. How do you dampen or tune an individual drum?

- Open the Drum Kit Designer from the Drummer Editor.
- Click on the drum you want to modify.
- Use the Dampen knob to reduce resonance and create a tighter sound.
- Use the Tune knob to adjust the pitch of the drum, making it higher or lower as needed.

27. How do you swap samples in Drum Machine Designer?

- Open the Drum Machine Designer by double-clicking the instrument on a drum track.
- Click on a drum pad to select it.
- In the Library pane, choose and load a different sample to replace the current one, customizing each pad for unique drum sounds.

28. How can you use audio effect plug-ins for an individual cell in the Drum Kit Designer?

- Open the Drum Kit Designer and select an individual drum piece.
- In the Mixer, each piece appears as a separate channel when using Multi-Output Mode.
- Add plug-ins (e.g., EQ, Compression, Reverb) directly to the channel strip of that drum piece, applying effects individually without affecting the entire kit.

THIRTEEN

UNDERSTANDING SMART CONTROLS, TRACK STACKS, KEY/ VELOCITY LIMITS, VOCODERS IN LOGIC

1. What are Smart Controls in Logic?

- Smart Controls provide a streamlined interface to control multiple plug-in parameters simultaneously. Each Smart Control can manipulate several parameters, such as EQ, reverb, and synth settings, through a single control knob or slider. This simplifies complex automation and allows quick adjustments during mixing and production.

2. How can you automate Smart Controls in Logic?

- Open the Smart Controls pane (press B).
- Assign parameters to a Smart Control.
- Press A to display the Automation view in the Tracks area.
- Select the Smart Control from the Automation parameter menu and draw or record automation by moving the Smart Control knob during playback.

3. How can you create your own Smart Controls in Logic?

- Open the Smart Controls pane (B).
- Click Learn in the Inspector.
- Move any software instrument or effect parameter to assign it.
- Adjust the knob, slider, or button style, and save your custom Smart Control for reuse.

4. Explain how you can delete one or all knobs that have parameters assigned to them.

- Open Smart Controls.
- Right-click the assigned knob and select Delete Assignment.
- To delete all, go to Edit > Delete All Assignments in the Smart Controls Inspector.

5. Provided with a software instrument, how can you control only half of the full range of the parameter using Smart Control?

- Open the Smart Controls pane and select the parameter.
- In the Parameter Mapping section, adjust the Min and Max values to limit the control range to half, allowing precise adjustments without full parameter sweeps.

6. How do you customise minimum and maximum values of a ranged parameter using Smart Controls?

- Select the assigned Smart Control.
- In the Parameter Mapping Inspector, set the Min and Max values, limiting the range to your desired control threshold, enhancing precision during automation.

7. How can you invert Smart Control parameters in Logic?

- In the Parameter Mapping Inspector, enable Invert Parameter.
- This flips the control response, making higher knob values decrease the parameter and vice versa, useful for creating inverse effects like filter sweeps.

8. What is the meaning of Scaling? Demonstrate with an example.

- Scaling adjusts the relationship between the Smart Control movement and the parameter response.

  - Example: A linear scale means equal control increments, while exponential scaling increases sensitivity at the higher end, ideal for precise fine-tuning near maximum values.

9. How can you assign an External MIDI Control Source with a Smart Control as destination?

- Open Smart Controls and click Learn.
- Move the physical control on your MIDI device (e.g., a knob on a MIDI controller).
- The Smart Control will now respond to the external MIDI control, allowing real-time hardware manipulation of software parameters.

10. Can we add arpeggiations using Smart Controls in Logic?

- Yes, assign a MIDI Arpeggiator to a Smart Control by:

  - Adding the Arpeggiator MIDI effect to a track.
  - Mapping Smart Controls to arpeggiator parameters (e.g., rate, octave range), allowing real-time arpeggio manipulation.

11. How can you take multi-outputs from Ultrabeat and EXS-24? What are the benefits of this function?

- Enable Multi-Output in the Track Inspector for Ultrabeat/EXS-24.
- Route individual outputs (kick, snare, hi-hat) to separate mixer channels.
- Benefits: Apply unique effects, EQ, and compression to each drum sound independently, enhancing mix clarity and creative control.

12. What is a Track Stack? How can you create a Track Stack in Logic?

- A Track Stack groups multiple tracks into one:

- ◦ Summing Stack: Combines audio/MIDI tracks into a single bus with shared processing.
- ◦ Folder Stack: Organizes tracks without merging audio.
- ◦ Creation: Select multiple tracks, right-click, and choose Create Track Stack, selecting either Summing or Folder Stack.

13. Create a track stack with three instruments and individually key limit them into separate octaves.

- Create a Summing Stack with three instrument tracks.
- In the Track Inspector, set the Key Range for each instrument (e.g., Bass: C1-B2, Strings: C3-B4, Lead: C5-B6).
- This ensures each instrument plays only within its assigned octave, allowing complex layered performances.

14. How can you do velocity limiting?

- Select a MIDI region, open the MIDI Transform window.
- Choose Limit Velocity, set the minimum and maximum values, and apply, ensuring all MIDI notes fall within the specified velocity range for consistent dynamics.

15. How do you create a robotic effect using vocoder?

- Insert EVOC 20 PolySynth (Logic's vocoder) on a software instrument track.
- Sidechain a vocal/audio input to the vocoder.
- Adjust the Formant, Harmonic, and Filter settings to create a classic robotic voice effect.

16. What type of track stack should you create to have MIDI regions on the main track trigger instruments on the sub-tracks?

- Use a Summing Stack, which allows a single MIDI region on the main stack track to trigger all instruments within the stack, ideal for layered synths or orchestral sections.

17. In the Smart Controls pane, how do you assign a screen control to a knob on your MIDI controller?

- Open Smart Controls and select the desired screen control.
- Click Learn, move the knob on your MIDI controller, and Logic will map the control, allowing hardware manipulation of software parameters.

FOURTEEN

HOW TO USE BUSSES IN LOGIC AND UNDERSTANDING SENDS

1. What are Aux tracks in Logic? How can you create these tracks?

- Aux tracks are auxiliary channels used for routing audio from multiple tracks to a single channel for shared processing (e.g., reverb, delay).

  - To create an Aux track:

    - Go to Mix > Create New Aux Channel Strip, or in the Mixer, create a Send on a track and Logic will automatically create an Aux track.
    - Name the Aux track (e.g., "Reverb Bus") and apply effects to it. Multiple tracks can send audio to this Aux for unified effect processing.

2. What are sends and inserts in Logic? How do you create them?

- Sends route audio from a track to an Aux channel, allowing parallel processing without altering the original track.

- To create: Open the Mixer, click on a track's Send slot, and select an available Bus. Adjust the send level to control how much signal is sent.

- Inserts apply effects (like EQ, compression) directly on a track's signal chain.

  - To create: In the Channel Strip, click an empty Insert slot and choose an effect plug-in.

3. What do you understand by the term parallel processing? Demonstrate with an example.

- Parallel processing involves blending a processed signal with the original signal for more control.
- Example:

  - Add a Compressor to an Aux track via a Send.
  - Set high compression on the Aux and blend it with the original, uncompressed track, preserving natural dynamics while enhancing punch.

4. How can you have a MIDI track play MIDI but have the audio being recorded in another track in Logic in real-time?

- Create a MIDI Instrument track and an Audio track.
- Set the Audio track input to the output of the MIDI Instrument track.
- Record-enable both tracks, and when you press Record, the MIDI track plays the instrument while the Audio track captures the sound in real-time.

5. Can you send multiple tracks to the same Bus? Also, can you route one track into multiple Busses? Demonstrate with examples.

- Yes, send multiple tracks to the same Bus by creating a Send on each track and selecting the same Bus number.
- One track to multiple Busses: Add several Send slots to one track and assign different Busses, e.g., one for reverb and another for delay, controlling each effect independently.

6. Explain the terms Pre-fader and Post-fader in terms of Logic's signal flow.

- Pre-fader: The signal is sent to the Bus before the track's fader, meaning changes to the track volume don't affect the send level. Used when you want a consistent send level regardless of track volume.
- Post-fader: The signal is sent after the fader, meaning any volume changes on the track also affect the send level, ideal for dynamic mix adjustments.

7. What is the signal flow of Logic from the audio region or MIDI instrument to the Fader in Logic? You can explain by drawing a diagram as well.

- Signal flow:

  - Audio/MIDI Region → Channel Insert Effects → Sends (Pre/Post-Fader) → Fader → Output (Stereo/Bus)

- Diagram Example:

  - [Audio Region] → [EQ] → [Compressor] → [Send to Bus (Reverb)] → [Fader] → [Stereo Out]

8. How do you route a multi-output drum instrument using Logic's signal routing capabilities?

- Insert a Multi-Output Drum Plugin (e.g., Ultrabeat).
- In the Mixer, click the + icon on the drum instrument track to create multiple outputs.
- Assign each drum piece (kick, snare, hi-hat) to separate outputs for individual mixing.

9. How do you make a sub-mix using busses in Logic?

- Select multiple tracks, create a Bus Send for each, and route them to a single Aux channel.

- This Aux acts as a sub-mix, allowing global control (volume, effects) for all routed tracks simultaneously.

10. What is gain staging? What are the various gain stages in Logic?

- Gain staging ensures audio levels are optimized at each stage of the signal path to prevent distortion or noise.
- Gain stages in Logic:

  - Audio Region Gain (adjustable in the Region Inspector)
  - Plugin Input/Output Gains
  - Track Fader Level
  - Bus/Aux Levels
  - Master Output Level

11. How do you do selection-based processing in Logic?

- Select an audio region, go to Functions > Selection-based Processing, and apply effects (EQ, reverb) to the selection only, leaving the rest of the track unaffected.

12. What is the use of the peak level meters on the faders in Logic?

- Peak level meters show the highest audio level of a track in real-time.
- Helps monitor for clipping (levels exceeding 0 dB), ensuring proper gain staging and avoiding distortion in the mix.

13. At what point does the fader meter in Logic turn from green to yellow and what does it mean?

- The fader meter turns yellow around -6 dB to 0 dB, indicating high signal levels approaching distortion.
- This is a warning to reduce gain to avoid clipping, which occurs when the signal goes above 0 dB (red).

FIFTEEN
ABLETON RACKS

1. What are Drum Racks?

- Drum Racks in Ableton Live are specialized instrument racks designed to host and sequence drum samples, one-shot sounds, and even synths. Each pad in the Drum Rack represents a MIDI note, triggering specific samples or instruments, making it ideal for beat-making and complex rhythm programming.

2. What are the ways in which we can create custom drum kits in Ableton and save them?

- Method 1: Load a Drum Rack, drag samples from the Browser onto the pads, and tweak them using built-in controls.
- Method 2: Use an empty Drum Rack, assign samples, and click the Save icon in the top-right of the device to store the custom kit in the User Library.

3. What is the incoming MIDI meter in the Drum Rack?

- The Incoming MIDI Meter displays real-time MIDI signal input when you trigger pads, confirming that MIDI notes are received and processed.

4. What is the Drum Rack Activator?

- The Activator is the power button that toggles the entire Drum Rack on or off, muting or activating all samples and effects within the rack simultaneously.

5. How many pads are there in a Drum Rack?

- A standard Drum Rack contains 128 pads, corresponding to the full range of MIDI notes (C-2 to G8), though only 16 are visible at a time.

6. What is the Scrolling Area for and how do we scroll in this region?

- The Scrolling Area allows navigation through the 128 pads. Use the up/down arrows on the rack or click and drag the vertical scroll bar on the right side to move through different sections.

7. What is the function of the output meter in Drum Rack?

- The Output Meter shows the audio signal level of each pad, ensuring the sound is audible and not clipping, and helping balance levels between samples.

8. How do we rename pads in a Drum Rack?

- Right-click any pad and select Rename.
- Type the new name and press Enter. This helps identify samples quickly during production.

9. How can we hotswap samples in a Drum Rack?

- Click the Hot-Swap icon (two arrows forming a circle) on any pad. This opens the Browser, allowing you to quickly swap the loaded sample with another while retaining all settings.

10. How can we mute/solo any pad in a Drum Rack?

- Each pad has its own Mute (M) and Solo (S) buttons. Click them directly to isolate or silence individual sounds within your drum pattern.

11. How can we trigger samples on a Drum Rack?

- Samples can be triggered using:

    ◦ A MIDI controller (like a Launchpad or MIDI keyboard).
    ◦ Computer keyboard mapped to MIDI notes.
    ◦ Clicking pads directly with the mouse in Session View or Piano Roll.

12. How can we copy samples in a Drum Rack?

- Drag a sample from one pad to another while holding Option (Mac) or Alt (Windows) to create a copy without removing the original.

13. How can we show/hide the chain list of a Drum Rack?

- Click the Chain button on the Drum Rack's left side to display or hide the Chain List, where each pad's signal chain (effects, routing) is managed.

14. How can we create Multis in a Drum Rack?

- Load multiple samples on a single pad using Instrument Racks within the Drum Rack.
- Assign different velocity or key ranges for layered drum sounds triggered simultaneously.

15. What are the functions of the chain list?

- The Chain List manages:

    ◦ Sample layers, allowing you to blend multiple sounds on one pad.
    ◦ Velocity ranges, determining which sample plays based on input strength.
    ◦ Routing options, sending each pad's audio to different tracks for independent processing.

16. What is the purpose of I/O and Sends and Returns on a Drum Rack?

- I/O (Input/Output): Assign individual pads to different outputs or receive MIDI from external sources.

- Sends/Returns: Add global effects (reverb, delay) to all or specific pads without applying them individually.

17. What is the purpose of Receive and Play functions?

- Receive: Accepts incoming MIDI signals to trigger pads.
- Play: Sends MIDI output from the Drum Rack to other devices or tracks.

18. What are choke groups and how do we use them?

- Choke Groups ensure that only one sound plays at a time within a group.

  - Example: Assign the hi-hat open and closed sounds to the same choke group so that playing one mutes the other, mimicking real drum behavior.

19. How do we repitch samples in the Drum Rack?

- Use the Transpose knob in the Sample section to change the pitch of any sample, adjusting it by semitones.

20. How do we add effects on different samples within the drum rack?

- Select a pad, click the Device View, and add effects (e.g., EQ Eight, Compressor) directly onto the pad's chain, affecting only that sample.

21. How can we add effects on the whole drum rack?

- Add effects to the Master Chain of the Drum Rack (found at the end of the chain list), applying them to all samples simultaneously.

22. How do we show/hide devices on a Drum Rack?

- Click the Device button in the bottom-left corner of the Drum Rack to toggle the Device View, displaying or hiding all loaded devices and effects.

23. What are Macros and how can we map them in Ableton?

- Macros are user-defined controls that manipulate multiple parameters at once.

    ◦ To map them, right-click any parameter in the Drum Rack, choose Map to Macro, and assign it to one of the 8 Macro knobs. This allows for dynamic, real-time control of complex settings.

24. How can we map multiple parameters on a single macro and invert their ranges?

- To map multiple parameters to a single Macro in Ableton:

    ◦ Right-click on any parameter and select Map to Macro 1 (or another Macro knob).
    ◦ Repeat this process for additional parameters.
    ◦ To invert ranges:
    ◦ Open the Macro Mapping Browser, adjust the Min/Max values, and click the Invert Range button for precise control over the parameter modulation.

25. How can we set the ranges of Macros?

- After mapping a parameter to a Macro, open the Macro Mapping panel and adjust the Min/Max range sliders to limit how much the Macro affects each mapped parameter.

26. How can we add/remove the number of Macros?

- Click the Configure button on the rack to add more Macros (up to 16 in Live 11+).
- To remove, right-click on a Macro and select Delete Macro.

27. How can we randomize macro values?

- Click the Randomize button on the top-right of the Macro panel, which instantly assigns random values to all active Macros, useful for creative sound design.

28. How can we create snapshots or variations of macro controls and recall them?

- Use the Macro Snapshots feature:

  - Set your Macros, click the camera icon to save the state, and recall by clicking the saved snapshot, ideal for live performances and quick variations.

29. How can we save a rack with assigned macros?

- After assigning Macros, click the Save icon (disk symbol) in the top-right of the device and store it in the User Library for future projects.

30. What is an Instrument Rack?

- An Instrument Rack is a collection of instruments and effects combined into a single device, enabling layered sounds, macro control, and complex signal chains within one track.

31. How can we layer instruments in an Instrument Rack?

- Add multiple instruments into an Instrument Rack's chain. Each chain acts like a separate track, all playing together, creating layered, rich sounds.

32. How do we control the volume and panning of individual chains in an Instrument Rack?

- Open the Chain List, adjust the Volume and Pan sliders for each chain independently, balancing each layer's contribution to the final sound.

33. What is the function of Key Limit Zones in an Instrument Rack? And what are the use of fades in Key Limit settings?

- Key Limit Zones restrict certain instruments to play only within specific MIDI note ranges.

- Fades allow smooth transitions between instruments when overlapping Key Zones.

34. What is the function of Velocity Limit Zones in an Instrument Rack?

- Velocity Zones trigger specific instruments or samples based on the incoming MIDI velocity, adding dynamic realism to performances.

35. What are the functions served by the chain selector editor in an Instrument Rack?

- The Chain Selector switches between different instrument chains using a single Macro knob, automating sound changes seamlessly within a set.

36. How can we add different effects to different instruments within an Instrument Rack?

- Drop effects directly onto each chain within the Instrument Rack, applying unique processing to each instrument.

37. How can we use Macro Control on Instrument Racks?

- Assign Macro knobs to control parameters across all instruments and effects in the rack, providing real-time modulation during live sets or automation in production.

38. How can we save custom Instrument Racks?

- Click the Save button on the Instrument Rack's interface and store it in the User Library for future use.

39. How can we hotswap instruments within the rack?

- Use the Hot-Swap button on any chain, opening the Browser for quick replacement of instruments without changing the rack structure.

40. What are audio effect racks?

- Audio Effect Racks combine multiple effects into one device, allowing layered processing, parallel chains, and macro-controlled modulation.

41. Give an example of a custom effect rack you can make in Ableton.

- Example: A Sidechain Compression Rack with a Compressor, EQ Eight, and Reverb, controlled by Macros for dynamic ducking and spatial effects.

42. How can we make a custom Dry/Wet knob using Audio Effect Racks?

- Create a Parallel Chain inside the effect rack: one with the effect and one dry. Assign a Macro to control the balance, creating a precise Dry/Wet knob.

43. How to use Macro Controls on Audio Effect Racks?

- Assign Macros to effect parameters (e.g., filter cutoff, reverb time) for intuitive control and automation during live performance or mixing.

44. How can we save/hotswap from an Audio Effect Rack?

- Save via the Save icon or Hot-Swap using the circular arrow button for quick effect replacement from the Browser.

45. What are MIDI effect racks in Ableton? What sets them apart from other racks?

- MIDI Effect Racks process MIDI data before it reaches instruments. They stand out as they control note sequences, velocity, pitch, and more, unlike other racks focused on audio processing.

46. Create a MIDI effect rack where notes below C4 are harmonized into chords and notes above C4 play arpeggios.

- Add a Chord MIDI effect to one chain with a Key Zone below C4 and an Arpeggiator to another chain above C4, creating a dynamic split MIDI instrument.

47. How can we use Macro Controls on MIDI effect racks?

- Assign Macros to control MIDI pitch, velocity, randomization, and more, enabling dynamic performance control over MIDI sequences.

48. How can we create a random melody generator using MIDI effect racks? Give an example.

- Add Random, Scale, and Arpeggiator MIDI effects in sequence. Adjust Random for note variation, Scale to keep notes in key, and Arpeggiator for rhythmic patterns, forming a random melody generator.

49. Make an instrument rack that has bass from C1 - B1, piano from C2 - B2, and strings from C3 - B3. Then save it.

- Create an Instrument Rack, add a Bass Synth with Key Limit C1-B1, a Piano Plugin with C2-B2, and a Strings Plugin with C3-B3. Adjust volumes, save as Multi-Instrument Layer.

50. Pick an audio drum loop of your choice. Convert it to MIDI in Ableton and use one of Ableton's stock kits to play it.

- Right-click the audio loop, select Convert Drums to New MIDI Track, and choose an Ableton Drum Kit from the Browser for playback and editing.

51. Pick an audio melody loop of your choice. Convert it to MIDI and use one of Ableton's stock instruments to play it.

- Right-click the melody loop, select Convert Melody to New MIDI Track, then load an Ableton Instrument (e.g., Electric Piano) for playback.

SIXTEEN

SIMPLER

1. How can we load audio directly within a Simpler in Ableton?

- There are three ways to load audio into Simpler:

  - Drag and Drop: Click and drag an audio file from Ableton's Browser or your computer directly into Simpler.
  - Resampling: Record or resample an audio track and drag it into Simpler.
  - Slice-to-Simpler: Right-click an audio clip and choose Slice to New MIDI Track, which opens the sample in Simpler.

2. What is a Simpler? What is it used for?

- Simpler is a lightweight sampling instrument in Ableton Live used to play, manipulate, and transform audio samples. It has three playback modes: Classic, 1-Shot, and Slice, each providing different ways to edit and trigger sounds.

3. How can we create an instrument from a tonal sample with Simpler?

- Load a tonal sample (e.g., a piano or synth note) into Simpler.
- Activate Warp Mode and enable Looping to sustain the sound.
- Use ADSR envelope settings for smooth attack and decay.
- Play across different pitches with a MIDI keyboard or Piano Roll to turn it into a playable instrument.

4. What are the characteristic features of Classic Mode?

- Looping Capabilities: The sample plays continuously when held.
- ADSR Envelope Control: Adjusts attack, decay, sustain, and release.
- Polyphony: Allows multiple notes to be played simultaneously.
- Filter and LFO Modulation: Shape the sound dynamically.

5. How can we turn short samples into pads using Simpler?

- Load a short vocal or synth sample into Simpler.
- Enable Looping and adjust the Loop Length for a smooth sustain.
- Apply Reverb, Delay, and Filtering for an atmospheric pad-like texture.

6. How can we crop samples within a Simpler?

- Use the Start and End markers to trim the sample.
- Click the Crop Sample button to permanently remove the unused sections.

7. What are the characteristic features of 1-Shot Mode in Simpler? How does it differ from the Classic Mode?

- 1-Shot Mode plays the sample once per trigger and ignores note length.
- Unlike Classic Mode, it does not support looping or ADSR shaping.

8. How can we activate Glide in Simpler?

- Click the Glide toggle in Simpler's Pitch section and adjust the Glide time to control the smoothness of pitch transitions.

9. What is the difference between Glide and Portamento?

- Glide: Affects only overlapping notes (legato-style transitions).
- Portamento: Applies pitch bending even when notes are not overlapping.

10. What are the characteristic features of the Slice Mode in Simpler?

- Automatically slices samples at transients or divisions.

- Each slice can be triggered by different MIDI notes.
- Offers manual slicing adjustments for precise sample triggering.

11. How do we control the ADSR in Simpler?

- Adjust Attack, Decay, Sustain, and Release using the Envelope section to shape the amplitude dynamics.

12. How can we double or halve the length of a sample within Simpler?

- Activate Warp Mode and use the Length parameter to expand or shorten playback speed.

13. How do we use warping in Simpler?

- Enable Warp Mode to stretch or manipulate the sample's timing while preserving pitch.

14. How can we hotswap from a Simpler?

- Click the Hot-Swap button (circular arrows) to quickly replace the sample from Ableton's Browser.

15. How can we control the overall volume of a Simpler?

- Adjust the Volume knob in Simpler's Main section or MIDI Velocity Sensitivity for dynamic response.

16. How can we transpose the sample within a Simpler?

- Use the Transpose knob to shift the pitch up or down in semitones.

17. How can we add pitch envelope in Simpler?

- Open the Pitch Envelope section, activate it, and adjust the Attack, Decay, and Amount for pitch modulation.

18. How can we save Simpler presets?

- Click the Save icon in Simpler's top-right corner and store the preset in Ableton's User Library.

SEVENTEEN
ROUTING IN ABLETON

1. What are the two types of processing we use in Ableton in terms of routing?

- The two main types of processing are:

  - Serial Processing: Audio is processed sequentially through a chain of effects, where each effect influences the next (e.g., EQ → Compressor → Reverb).
  - Parallel Processing: Audio is split and processed through multiple chains simultaneously, allowing different effects on each chain before being recombined (e.g., a dry signal mixed with a compressed one for punch).

2. Explain the signal flow of a MIDI and Audio track in Ableton with the help of a diagram.

- Signal Flow for MIDI Track:

  - MIDI Input → MIDI Effects → Instrument Device → Audio Effects → Mixer Output

- Signal Flow for Audio Track:

  - Audio Input → Audio Effects → Mixer Output

3. What is Serial Processing?

- Serial Processing refers to applying effects one after another in a linear sequence. Each effect processes the output of the previous one, crucial for signal-dependent effects like EQ before compression.

4. Explain all the methods of Serial Processing within Ableton.

- Single Chain in Device View: Adding effects one after another on a single track.
- Racks for Layered Serial Processing: Using Instrument or Audio Effect Racks to process chains in series.
- Insert Effects on Tracks: Placing effects directly on a track's insert section.

5. How do we group tracks in Ableton?

- Select multiple tracks, right-click, and choose Group Tracks.
- The grouped track (a Bus) lets you control volume, effects, and routing collectively.

6. What are nested groups?

- Nested Groups are groups within groups. For example, a Drum Group containing Kick, Snare, Hi-Hat tracks, each with its own effects, and the entire drum set processed through the main group.

7. What is Parallel Processing?

- Parallel Processing duplicates the signal and processes each copy differently before recombining them. For example, using a dry signal with a heavily compressed version to maintain natural dynamics while adding punch.

8. How can we a regular audio track as an Aux track in Ableton?

- Change the track's Input Type to No Input and Audio To to a Return Track, using it as an Aux track for effects like reverb or delay.

9. What is a Return Track and how can we add Return Tracks in Ableton?

- A Return Track is a dedicated channel for effects processing that multiple tracks can send audio to.

  - To add: Right-click in the Session View's Mixer area and select Insert Return Track.

10. Define Pre FX, Post FX, and Post Mixer with the help of a diagram.

- Pre FX: Sends audio before any effect processing.
- Post FX: Sends audio after effect processing.
- Post Mixer: Sends audio after the track's volume and pan adjustments.
- (Diagrams in Ableton's Routing Matrix show these points clearly.)

11. What are gain stages? How many gain stages are there in Ableton?

- Gain Stages are points where the signal's volume can be adjusted.

  - In Ableton: Input Gain, Clip Gain, Device Gain, Track Volume, Return Track Volume, and Master Output Volume (6 stages).

12. How can we process specific frequency bands by using sends and returns?

- Add an EQ Eight on a Return Track, isolate a frequency band, and apply effects like Reverb. Tracks sending to this Return will process only the selected band.

13. Create a valley type sound effect using return tracks.

- Add a Return Track with a Notch Filter (EQ Eight), automate the filter sweep, and combine it with Delay for a valley-like echo effect.

14. How can we create a parallel master bus in Ableton?

- Duplicate the Master Track with effects like Compression and EQ, and blend it with the original output for parallel processing.

15. What is resampling and how is it used?

- Resampling records the output of any track back into Ableton.

  - Add an Audio Track, set Input to Resampling, and record. This is used for committing effects to audio or creating loops.

16. How can we sidechain with third-party plugins in Ableton?

- Load a plugin like FabFilter Pro-C, select the Sidechain Input, and route an audio source (e.g., a kick) from Ableton's track routing panel.

17. How can we use sends and returns on a Drum Rack?

- Open the Drum Rack's Chain List, add a Return Chain, and assign sends from individual drum pads to the Return Chain for specific effects.

18. Can we send signal from the drum rack to return tracks? If yes then explain how. Demonstrate two methods.

- Method 1: Use the Drum Rack Chain List, enable sends, and route to a Return Track.
- Method 2: Route the Audio Output of the entire Drum Rack to a Return Track using the main track's routing panel.

19. What are the routing options for Return Tracks in Ableton?

- Return Tracks can be routed to Master Output, Other Return Tracks, or External Outputs using the Audio To section.

20. How to parallel process using audio effect racks?

- Create multiple chains within an Audio Effect Rack (e.g., one chain with compression and another dry), adjusting levels for parallel processing.

21. How can we use Drum Racks as a multi-output device in Ableton?

- Enable External Outputs for each pad in the Drum Rack Chain List, sending each drum to a separate track for individual processing.

22. How can we parallel process the Instruments within an Instrument Rack?

- Add multiple chains within an Instrument Rack, apply different effects to each chain, and blend them using volume levels.

23. How can we Freeze and Flatten tracks in Ableton?

- Right-click on a track and choose Freeze Track (renders the track with effects). Then, right-click again and select Flatten to convert it into audio.

24. How can we use Turntable effects in Ableton without any plugins?

- Use Clip Envelopes to manually adjust the Transpose knob or automate the Vinyl Distortion Device for scratching effects.

25. What is the purpose of a Freeze Tail?

- Freeze Tail preserves reverb, delay, or any long-tail effects when freezing a track, ensuring that sustained effects are not cut off during playback or export.

EIGHTEEN

WORKING WITH AUTOMATIONS AND UNDERSTANDING GLOBAL CONTROLS IN LOGIC

1. What do you understand by Automations? What is its shortcut in Logic?

- Automation in Logic Pro refers to the process of recording and manipulating changes in a track over time, such as volume, panning, effects, and plugin parameters.

  - Shortcut: Press A on your keyboard to open the Automation View in Logic.

2. Explain the following types of Automations: i) Online Automation, ii) Offline Automation, iii) Track Automation, iv) Region Automation.

- Online Automation: Automation recorded in real-time as you adjust parameters during playback.
- Offline Automation: Drawn or programmed manually without playback, using the Automation Lanes.

- Track Automation: Automation applied to an entire track, affecting all regions on that track.
- Region Automation: Applied to specific regions, independent of the track's automation settings.

3. Explain the differences between Touch Mode Automation and Latch Mode Automation in Logic.

- Touch Mode: Adjusts parameters when you click and hold; once released, it returns to the previous value.
- Latch Mode: Adjusts parameters when clicked, but once released, it stays at the adjusted value until manually changed.

4. Explain how Read Mode works while working with automations in Logic.

- Read Mode plays back all recorded automation data without allowing new automation changes. It's used for review and playback of existing automation.

5. Explain how Write Mode works while working with automations in Logic.

- Write Mode records automation data every time the track is played, overwriting any existing automation on that track.

6. How do you copy Track Automation into Region Automation in Logic? Also explain how to do the reverse.

- Copy Track to Region: Select the track, go to Mix > Convert Automation and choose Track to Region Automation.
- Reverse: Select the region, then choose Region to Track Automation from the same menu.

7. How can you add an automated region to your loop library?

- Select the region, right-click, and choose Add to Loop Library. Automation data is saved with the loop for future use.

8. How can you copy Automations from one track to another in Logic?

- Select the automation data using the Marquee Tool, copy (Command + C), then paste (Command + V) onto the new track's automation lane.

9. How can you perform offline/online Automations in Logic?

- Offline: Use the Automation Lanes manually in the editor.
- Online: Adjust parameters during playback while in Latch, Touch, or Write Mode.

10. How can you trim the Automation range in Logic?

- Open the Automation View, select the range using the Marquee Tool, and drag the automation points to adjust the range.

11. How do you do the following in Logic: i) Copy Automation, ii) Curve Automation, iii) Select Automation

- Copy Automation: Select automation points, press Command + C to copy, and Command + V to paste.
- Curve Automation: Hold Control + Shift and drag a line between two points to create a curve.
- Select Automation: Click on any point or line in the automation lane using the Pointer Tool.

12. Describe all methods of deleting Automation from Logic.

- Select automation points and press Delete.
- Right-click the automation line and choose Delete Automation.
- Use the Eraser Tool to click on automation points.

13. How many copy the automation path of a parameter in a track to a different parameter in the same track?

- Select the automation points, copy them, then switch to the new parameter in the automation lane and paste.

14. How can create and delete Automation Nodes?

- Create: Click on the automation line with the Pointer Tool to add a node.
- Delete: Click a node and press Delete or use the Eraser Tool.

15. How can you do quick access automation in Logic?

- Press A to access automation lanes quickly, or use the Automation Quick Access in the Preferences > Automation section.

16. Describe what you understand by Snap Automation.

- Snap Automation ensures that automation points align precisely with the grid, beats, or specific intervals for accuracy.

17. How can you perform stepper type automations in Logic?

- Use the Step Editor to assign values at each step or interval, creating rhythmic automation changes.

18. What is the purpose of a Subtrack Disclosure Triangle?

- This triangle, next to a track, reveals automation lanes or subtracks (e.g., for volume, pan, and plugin parameters).

19. In Logic, how can you change the time signature of a project from 4/4 to 3/4?

- Open the Signature List from the Global Tracks, click the + icon, and set the new time signature (e.g., 3/4).

20. How can you automate master tempo in Logic?

- Enable the Tempo Track from the Global Tracks, then draw automation points for tempo changes.

21. How can you create and adjust markers in Logic?

- Use the Marker Track from Global Tracks, click the + icon to add a marker, and drag it to adjust its position.

22. How can you assign any parameter to any external MIDI Controller control?

- Open Logic Remote or Controller Assignments, select the parameter, and move a control on your MIDI device to link them.

23. How can you load a movie into Logic?

- Go to File > Movie > Open Movie, select the file, and it will appear on the timeline.

24. How can you create Automations by using external hardware midi controllers?

- In Latch or Touch Mode, move your hardware controller knobs or faders during playback, and Logic will record the automation.

25. What are Group Automations and what are its benefits?

- Group Automation applies automation to a group of tracks simultaneously, saving time and ensuring consistency (e.g., applying the same volume fade to all drum tracks).

26. How do you do Region Automations in Logic?

- Select a region, open the Automation View, and choose Region Automation from the drop-down menu.

27. How can you automate sends in Logic?

- In the Automation Lane, choose the Send Level parameter, and draw automation points to increase or decrease send levels.

28. How do you automate Aux tracks in Logic?

- Select the Aux Track, open the Automation Lane, and automate parameters like volume, pan, or effects.

29. How can side chain a track in Logic? Show with an example.

- Add a Compressor on a track, enable Side Chain Input, and select the kick drum track as the input. The audio will "duck" when the kick plays, creating a rhythmic effect.

NINETEEN

AUTOMATION IN ABLETON

1. How to turn Automation on/off using a shortcut?

- In Ableton Live, automation can be quickly enabled or disabled using the keyboard shortcut A. Pressing A toggles the automation mode, showing or hiding the automation lanes for each track. When enabled, all existing automation curves become visible, and new automation can be drawn or edited. Turning it off allows you to focus solely on the arrangement without the distraction of automation lines.

2. What function does the drop-down menus on each track serve when Automation is turned on?

- When automation is activated, each track in Ableton Live displays a drop-down menu that allows users to select the specific parameter they wish to automate. This can include volume, pan, sends, device controls, and third-party plugin parameters. Selecting an option from this menu reveals the automation lane for that parameter, where users can draw, edit, or delete automation curves to control the parameter over time.

3. How can we use Automation Lanes?

- Automation lanes in Ableton Live are used to create, edit, and manage automation for various track parameters. To use them:

- ◦ Enable Automation View by pressing A.
- ◦ Click on the drop-down menu in the track header to select the desired parameter.
- ◦ Draw automation by clicking and dragging with the mouse or using the pencil tool (shortcut B).
- ◦ Add multiple lanes by clicking the small plus sign below an existing lane to automate additional parameters on the same track.

4. How can we create a node on an Automation curve and how can we delete it?

- To create a node: Click anywhere on an automation curve while holding Ctrl (Windows) or Cmd (Mac). This adds a breakpoint or node that can be dragged to adjust the automation.
- To delete a node: Click on the node and press Delete or right-click and select Delete. Multiple nodes can be selected and deleted simultaneously by dragging a selection box around them.

5. How can we bypass snap to grid for automation nodes?

- Hold down Ctrl (Windows) or Cmd (Mac) while dragging a node. This bypasses the snap-to-grid feature, allowing for precise placement of automation nodes at any point on the timeline, rather than being restricted to grid divisions.

6. How can we create steps using Pencil Tool?

- Activate the Pencil Tool by pressing B.
- Click and drag horizontally across the automation lane to draw step-like automation curves. Each step corresponds to the grid division, making it useful for creating rhythmic automation changes such as volume gating or filter modulation.

7. How can we free draw automations using Pencil Tool?

- With the Pencil Tool (shortcut B) enabled, simply click and drag freely across the automation lane. This method ignores grid lines and allows you to draw smooth, continuous curves, ideal for gradual parameter changes like pitch bends or volume fades.

8. What does simplify envelope do?

- The Simplify Envelope function reduces the number of breakpoints in an automation curve while maintaining its overall shape. This is useful for cleaning up complex automation to make editing easier. Right-click on the automation line and select Simplify Envelope to apply this feature.

9. How do we enter specific values for Nodes?

- Double-click on a node to bring up a small box where you can manually enter a precise value. Alternatively, right-click on the node and select Edit Value. This ensures exact parameter control, crucial for tasks requiring high precision, such as pitch or tempo adjustments.

10. What are the ways in which we can trim automation?

- Drag the automation line up or down to adjust the overall level while preserving the shape.
- Select nodes and use the arrow keys to nudge the entire selection.
- Right-click and choose Scale Automation to proportionally increase or decrease the values.
- Use the automation handle at the top of the lane to trim the entire envelope collectively.

11. How can we revert or invert automations?

- Revert Automation: Right-click on an automation lane and select Revert to Last Value. This resets the automation to its previously recorded state.
- Invert Automation: Select the automation curve, right-click, and choose Invert Automation. This flips the automation vertically, making high values low and vice versa, which is useful for creating contrasting modulation effects.

12. How to adjust the degree of curvature on an automation line?

- Hold Shift while clicking and dragging an automation segment. This bends the line into a curve, allowing you to create smooth transitions rather than linear changes.

13. How can we delete automations?

- Single Node: Click on the node and press Delete.
- Entire Curve: Select the automation curve by clicking and dragging, then press Delete.
- Specific Parameter Automation: Right-click on the automation lane and select Clear Envelope.

14. What is the function of Re-enable Automation button, when does it get activated?

- The Re-enable Automation button appears in the transport bar when manual adjustments override existing automation. Clicking this button restores the previously recorded automation, ensuring that manual tweaks don't permanently alter the automation data.

15. How can we add Automation lanes manually?

- Press A to show automation.
- Click the + icon at the bottom of an existing lane to add more lanes for different parameters, such as volume, pan, or effect controls.

16. What is the purpose of Lock Envelope button in Ableton?

- The Lock Envelope button ensures that automation remains linked to the timeline position, not to the audio clip. This means that even if you move or copy the clip, the automation stays in its original place, maintaining precise control over your parameters.

17. How can we record Automation in Ableton?

- Arm the Track by clicking the small arm button (red circle).
- Press Automation Arm (next to the record button).

- Play the session and tweak the desired parameter in real-time. Ableton captures all adjustments as automation data.

18. What are the ways in which we can duplicate or copy automations?

- Copy/Paste: Select the automation, press Ctrl/Cmd + C, and paste it with Ctrl/Cmd + V.
- Drag + Alt: Hold Alt while dragging the automation to create a duplicate.
- Duplicate Command: Select the automation region and press Ctrl/Cmd + D to duplicate it immediately.

19. How can we copy automations to another track?

- Select the automation curve.
- Press Ctrl/Cmd + C to copy.
- Select the target track's automation lane and press Ctrl/Cmd + V to paste it, ensuring seamless parameter control across multiple tracks.

20. How do we automate third-party plugins?

- Open the third-party plugin.
- Click on the small triangle icon in the track's device view to display available parameters.
- Move the desired parameter; it will appear in the Configure panel.
- Automate it by drawing curves in the automation lane just like native Ableton controls.

21. What are a few examples of Clip Envelope Automation?

- Volume Fade: Automate volume levels within a clip.
- Pitch Bend: Create pitch glides for audio or MIDI clips.
- Filter Sweeps: Automate frequency cutoff for dynamic effects.
- Panning: Move sound from left to right over time, adding spatial dimension.

22. How can we add specific parameter changes to specific clips using clip automation?

- Double-click the clip to open the Clip View.
- Click the Envelope Box to choose the parameter you wish to automate.
- Draw automation directly in the clip, which will move with the clip when rearranged, perfect for precise, localized changes.

23. What is Modulation and how is it different from Automation?

- Modulation: Adds additional movement on top of existing automation, creating more complex and dynamic changes without overwriting the original automation.
- Automation: Directly controls a parameter over time with defined curves and breakpoints.

24. What is the difference between region linked and region unlinked modulation?

- Region Linked Modulation: Stays within the clip and moves with it.
- Region Unlinked Modulation: Independent of the clip's position and remains fixed in the timeline, useful for global changes across a session.

25. How to add pre-made automation curves in Ableton?

- Right-click on an automation lane and select Insert Shape to choose from a set of pre-made curves, such as sine waves, ramps, or pulses, saving time and adding professional polish.

26. Can we copy automation for MIDI on/off controls to MIDI CC controls?

- Yes. Select the MIDI on/off automation.
- Copy it using Ctrl/Cmd + C.
- Paste it into a MIDI CC lane, ensuring the timing and shape are retained, allowing for detailed control over MIDI devices.

TWENTY

EXTRA QUESTIONS FOR ABLETON

1. How can we create a Sine Wave in Ableton?

- Creating a sine wave in Ableton can be done using the following methods:

  - Operator Instrument:

    - Open Ableton Live and create a new MIDI track.
    - Drag and drop the Operator instrument from the Instruments section of the browser.
    - In the Operator settings, select the waveform for the oscillator. Choose Sine Wave from the dropdown menu.
    - Draw MIDI notes in the Piano Roll to generate a pure sine wave tone.

  - Analog Instrument:

    - Add the Analog instrument to a MIDI track.
    - In the oscillator section, select Sine as the waveform for Oscillator 1.
    - Adjust the amplitude envelope and filter settings as necessary.

  - Max for Live Devices: Use devices like LFO or Sine Modulator to generate continuous sine wave modulations. This produces a clean, smooth sine wave sound, commonly used in sub-bass, pads, and melodic lines.

2. How can we invert phase of a signal in Ableton?

- Inverting the phase of a signal helps correct phase cancellation issues:

  - Utility Device Method:

    - Add the Utility effect to an audio or MIDI track.
    - In the Utility settings, find the Phase buttons labeled L and R.
    - Click on these buttons to invert the phase of the left, right, or both channels.

  - Audio Clip Method:

    - Double-click an audio clip.
    - In the Sample Editor, right-click and select Invert Phase from the menu. This is useful in mixing to prevent phase cancellation when layering sounds.

3. What are the functions the Utility plugin in Ableton serve?

- The Utility plugin is versatile and offers several functions:

  - Gain Control: Adjust the volume of a track without affecting the mixer fader.
  - Panning: Control the stereo positioning of a signal.
  - Phase Inversion: Invert the phase of left, right, or both channels.
  - Stereo Width Adjustment: Modify the stereo field from mono to wide stereo.
  - DC Offset Correction: Remove unwanted DC offsets in audio signals. This tool is essential for gain staging, phase alignment, and stereo imaging.

4. What is the best way to automate track panning and track volume?

- Automation adds dynamic movement to mixes:

- ◦ Panning Automation:

  - In the Arrangement View, click on the Automation button.
  - Select the Panning parameter from the drop-down menu on the track header.
  - Draw automation curves using the Draw Tool to move sound between left and right channels.

- ◦ Volume Automation:

  - In Arrangement View, select the track's Volume parameter.
  - Draw automation points to create fades, swells, and dynamic volume changes.

- ◦ Session View Automation:

  - Use the Envelopes section in the Clip View to draw panning or volume automation within individual clips.

5. How can we turn a stereo signal into a mono signal in Ableton?

- To convert stereo to mono:

- ◦ Utility Device Method:

  - Insert a Utility plugin on the desired track.
  - Adjust the Width control to 0% for a fully mono signal.

- ◦ Audio Effect Rack Method:

  - Create an Audio Effect Rack.
  - Duplicate the signal into two chains and pan them both to center.

- ◦ Resampling Method:

  - Create a new audio track and set its input to the original track.
  - Record the signal while enabling Mono Input in the track settings. This ensures compatibility across different playback systems.

6. What is the purpose of the Bass Mono button?

- The Bass Mono button ensures that low frequencies are summed to mono:

  - Located in the Utility Plugin, this button ensures that frequencies below a set threshold are played in mono.
  - Purpose:

    - Prevents phase issues in bass frequencies.
    - Ensures compatibility with mono playback systems like clubs.
    - Enhances the clarity and punch of low-end frequencies.

7. How to invert phase of only the left or right channel?

- Utility Plugin:

  - Add the Utility device to a track.
  - Click the Phase L button to invert only the left channel or Phase R for the right channel. This helps in stereo imaging adjustments without affecting both channels simultaneously.

8. How can we use Ableton's stock compressor for sidechaining?

- Sidechaining creates dynamic rhythm and space:
- Steps:

  - Add Compressor to the track you want to sidechain.
  - Expand the Compressor View by clicking the arrow.
  - Enable the Sidechain button.
  - Choose the input track (e.g., Kick drum) from the drop-down menu.
  - Adjust the Threshold, Ratio, Attack, and Release settings to achieve the desired pumping effect. This technique is widely used in electronic music for ducking effects.

9. Which plugins support sidechaining in Ableton?

- Ableton's stock and third-party plugins that support sidechaining include:

  - Ableton Stock Plugins:

    - Compressor
    - Multiband Dynamics
    - Gate

  - Third-Party Plugins:

    - FabFilter Pro-C 2
    - Waves C1 Compressor
    - Xfer LFO Tool Sidechaining allows dynamic interaction between audio tracks for a polished mix.

10. What is a Vocoder and how can it be used in Ableton?

- A Vocoder modulates audio signals:

  - Function:

    - Modulates the sound of one signal (carrier) using another (modulator).

  - Usage in Ableton:

    - Add the Vocoder to a vocal track.
    - Set the Carrier to an internal synth or external input.
    - Adjust bands, formant, and release settings for robotic, harmonized effects. Vocoders are used for electronic vocals, robotic voices, and texture layers.

11. What is the difference between Solo and Solo In Place?

- Solo: Mutes all other tracks except the selected one.
- Solo In Place: Solos a track within its context, including send effects and group processing.

12. What is the purpose of split stereo pan mode?

- Split Stereo Pan Mode: Provides independent control over left and right channel panning.
- Purpose:

  - Allows precise stereo positioning.
  - Balances stereo fields without collapsing to mono.

13. How can we solo bands in Ableton's EQ Eight?

- Steps:

  - Add EQ Eight to a track.
  - Click the Headphone Icon next to each band to solo the selected frequency band. This helps isolate and fine-tune specific frequency ranges during mixing.

14. What does the EQ Eight do?

- EQ Eight is an eight-band equalizer with the following features:

  - Frequency Bands: 8 adjustable frequency bands.
  - Filter Types: High-pass, low-pass, notch, bell, and shelving filters.
  - Spectral Analysis: Real-time visual feedback of audio frequencies.
  - Applications:

    - Sculpting sound.
    - Removing unwanted frequencies.
    - Enhancing specific elements in the mix.

15. How can we expand the spectrum analyzer of EQ Eight in Ableton?

- Steps:

  - Open EQ Eight on a track.
  - Click the Expand button next to the analyzer display to enlarge the spectrum view. This provides a more detailed analysis of frequency

content.

16. How can we attenuate frequencies using an EQ?

- Attenuating frequencies means reducing the amplitude of specific frequency ranges:

  - Steps in Ableton EQ Eight:

    - Add EQ Eight to the track.
    - Select a frequency band by clicking on one of the eight points.
    - Adjust the Gain knob downwards to reduce the volume of the selected frequency.
    - Use the Q control to narrow or widen the frequency range affected.

  - Practical Usage:

    - Remove unwanted resonances (e.g., harsh highs).
    - Control muddiness by attenuating low-mid frequencies.
    - Tame sibilance by cutting frequencies around 5kHz–8kHz.

17. What is the purpose of Q in EQ Eight?

- The Q factor controls the bandwidth of frequencies affected by an EQ band:

  - Higher Q Values:

    - Narrow bandwidth.
    - Precise adjustments (e.g., removing specific resonances).

  - Lower Q Values:

    - Wide bandwidth.
    - Broad tonal changes (e.g., overall warmth enhancement). In EQ Eight, adjusting the Q helps balance between precision and subtlety in equalization tasks.

18. How can we tune samples in Ableton?

- Tuning samples ensures they match the key of your project:

  - Using Simpler/Sampler:

    - Load the sample into Simpler.
    - Adjust the Transpose knob to pitch the sample up or down in semitones.
    - Fine-tune using the Detune control (in cents).

  - Using the Clip Editor:

    - Double-click the audio sample.
    - In the Sample Editor, adjust the Transpose setting.

  - Tip: Use Tuner from Ableton's devices to visually check the pitch of the sample.

19. What purpose does the device Spectrum serve?

- Spectrum is a real-time frequency analyzer:

  - Functions:

    - Displays the frequency content of an audio signal.
    - Provides visual feedback for identifying peaks, dips, and overall frequency balance.

  - Applications:

    - Balancing mix frequencies.
    - Identifying problematic frequencies (e.g., harsh resonances).
    - Ensuring proper distribution of lows, mids, and highs in a mix.

20. What are .asd files and how are they created?

- .asd Files (Ableton Sample Analysis Data) store metadata for audio files:

- ○ Warp settings.
- ○ Loop points.
- ○ Gain adjustments.

- Created When:

  - ○ An audio file is imported into Ableton.
  - ○ Ableton analyzes and saves the file's settings automatically. These files ensure that audio files retain their warp and playback settings when reopened.

21. What are .alc files and how are they created in Ableton?

- .alc files stand for Ableton Live Clip files. These files store audio or MIDI clip information including device settings, automation, and warp markers. They act as a shortcut to instantly reuse clips with all their parameters intact, without saving an entire project or device rack.
- Features of .alc files:

  - ○ Retains the clip's MIDI or audio data, along with:

    - ▪ Warp settings.
    - ▪ Clip envelopes (such as pitch, volume, or effects automation).
    - ▪ Any applied effects or instruments within the track.
    - ▪ Loop points and playback position.

  - ○ Provides a way to drag and drop complex clips into future projects without re-creating settings from scratch.

- How to Create .alc Files:

  - ○ Select the Clip:

    - ▪ Choose an audio or MIDI clip from the Session View or Arrangement View.
    - ▪ Drag to Browser:

- Drag the clip directly to the Ableton Browser on the left side (under Places).
- This automatically creates an .alc file in the selected folder.

- Save via Right-Click:

  - Right-click on the clip.
  - Choose "Export Clip as .alc".
  - Select a location in the browser to save the clip.

- Uses of .alc Files:

  - Quickly load commonly used loops, samples, or MIDI patterns into new projects.
  - Maintain consistent automation and effect settings across multiple projects.
  - Build a library of ready-to-use musical ideas and templates.

- Example:

  - You have a perfect drum loop with EQ, compression, and warp settings.
  - Saving it as an .alc allows you to drag it into any new session, retaining all those precise settings immediately.
  - This format is especially helpful for streamlining workflows, saving time, and maintaining high production standards consistently.

22. What are .alp files and how are they created?

- .alp Files (Ableton Live Packs) are compressed project files:

  - Contain audio, MIDI, device settings, and project configurations.

- Created When:

  - Exporting a project as a Live Pack via File > Manage Project > Create Pack.
  - Useful for sharing or archiving complete Ableton sessions.

23. What is the difference between a .adg and a .adv file?

- .adg (Ableton Device Group): Saves an entire device rack, including chains, effects, and instruments.
- .adv (Ableton Device Preset): Saves individual device settings, such as an EQ or compressor preset. Both are essential for saving and recalling sound designs and effect setups efficiently.

24. How can Ableton detect the tempo of an incoming signal?

- Using Warp Mode:

  - Import an audio file.
  - Double-click to open the Clip View.
  - Click Warp and select Auto for Ableton to analyze and set the tempo.

- Tapping Method:

  - Play the signal.
  - Use the Tap Tempo button in the top control bar to manually set the tempo.

- Using External Inputs:

  - Ableton can also sync to external MIDI clock signals for detecting and aligning tempos.

TWENTY-ONE
LIVE LOOPS IN LOGIC PRO.

1. What are Live Loops and how are they used in Logic?

- Live Loops is a grid-based environment in Logic Pro designed for non-linear music composition and performance. It allows users to trigger individual cells containing loops, MIDI patterns, audio recordings, or even entire scenes, enabling real-time experimentation with musical ideas. This tool is especially useful for live performances, as it facilitates improvisation without altering the linear timeline of the main project. Users can capture spontaneous performances and later arrange them into the main project's timeline for further refinement.

2. What is the Live Loop Grid?

- The Live Loop Grid is a visual interface in Logic Pro that organizes loops and samples into rows and columns. Each cell within the grid can contain a loop or musical element that can be triggered independently or as part of a group called a scene. Rows represent tracks, while columns represent different sections or ideas within a project. This grid system helps musicians build complex arrangements dynamically during both production and live performances.

3. How do you show/hide Live Loops Grid?

- To show or hide the Live Loops Grid in Logic Pro:

- ○ Show: Click the Live Loops button on the Control Bar, which is represented by a grid icon, or use the shortcut Shift + L.
- ○ Hide: Click the same button or press Shift + L again to return to the traditional timeline view.

- This toggle allows seamless switching between grid-based and timeline-based workflows.

4. How to create a Live Loops Project in Logic from a grid template?

- To create a Live Loops Project using a grid template:

  - ○ Open Logic Pro and select File > New from Template.
  - ○ Choose the Live Loops category.
  - ○ Select a pre-designed grid template or an empty grid template based on your needs.
  - ○ Click Choose to open the project. This template provides a ready-made grid with preloaded loops, simplifying the process of starting a Live Loops session.

5. How to start/stop Live Loops in Logic Pro?

- Start a Live Loop: Click the Play button on any cell or scene in the grid.
- Stop a Live Loop: Click the cell or scene again to stop playback, or press Spacebar to stop all loops. Alternatively, use the Stop button in the Control Bar to halt all playback within the Live Loops Grid.

6. What are cells and how do you start/stop them?

- Cells in Live Loops are individual containers that hold audio, MIDI, or automation data.

  - ○ To start a cell, simply click on it, and it will begin playing in sync with the project tempo.
  - ○ To stop a cell, click it again or press the Stop button in the grid. Cells can be looped indefinitely or set to play only once, depending on the desired performance.

7. Show how you can queue a cell in Logic Pro?

- To queue a cell:

    - Right-click on a cell and select Queue from the contextual menu.
    - Alternatively, hold Shift while clicking multiple cells to queue them.
    - The queued cells will flash, indicating they are ready to play at the next available beat or bar, maintaining synchronization within the project.

8. What is the use of Quantize Start Value?

- The Quantize Start Value ensures that cells in Live Loops start playing in time with the project's tempo.

    - It sets a grid reference (e.g., 1/4 note, 1/8 note) so that when you trigger a cell, it aligns perfectly with the nearest beat, preventing any timing issues during playback.

9. How to set Quantize Start Value for a cell?

- To set the Quantize Start Value:

    - Select a cell.
    - Open the Cell Inspector by clicking the 'i' icon.
    - Under Quantize Start, choose the desired rhythmic value (e.g., 1/16, 1/8). This ensures the selected cell triggers at the exact specified beat division within the project.

10. How to add a region from the tracks area to the Live Loops Grid?

- To add a region:

    - Select the region in the Tracks Area.
    - Drag it into an empty cell in the Live Loops Grid. This action creates a copy of the region within the grid, allowing it to be triggered independently from the main timeline.

11. How to convert drummer patterns to cells in Logic Pro?

- To convert drummer patterns:

    ◦ Select the Drummer track containing the pattern.
    ◦ Drag the drummer region into an empty cell in the Live Loops Grid.
    ◦ Logic will automatically convert the drummer pattern into a MIDI region within the cell, retaining the rhythm and feel of the original drummer track.

12. What is a Scene in Logic? How is it used?

- A Scene in Logic Pro is a column in the Live Loops Grid that triggers all the cells in that column simultaneously.

    ◦ Usage: Scenes allow you to play multiple loops at once, creating an entire musical section.
    ◦ Click the Scene trigger button at the bottom of a column to start playback of all cells within that column, making it easy to build sections like verses, choruses, or drops.

13. How can we edit cells in Logic?

- To edit cells:

    ◦ Double-click on a cell to open the Cell Editor.
    ◦ Edit audio with tools like trim, fade, and quantize.
    ◦ Edit MIDI by adjusting notes, velocities, and automation within the Piano Roll.
    ◦ You can also add effects, adjust pitch, and change playback settings from the Inspector.

14. What does the Play mode option do in a cell? What are the different play modes and how do they behave?

- The Play Mode determines how a cell behaves when triggered:

    ◦ Loop: Repeats the cell content continuously.

- ◦ One-shot: Plays the cell content once without looping.
- ◦ Reverse: Plays the content backward.
- ◦ Gate: Plays only while the cell trigger is held. Each mode provides flexibility in how loops and samples are performed and manipulated in real time.

15. How can we change the Start Behaviour of a cell?

- To change the start behavior:

  - ◦ Select the cell and open the Cell Inspector.
  - ◦ Adjust the Start Offset to shift the playback start point.
  - ◦ Set the Launch Quantization to define how quickly the cell responds after being triggered (e.g., immediately, on the next beat/bar).

16. How to copy/paste regions to cells in the Live Loops Grid?

- Select the region from the Tracks Area.
- Press Command + C to copy.
- Click on an empty cell in the grid and press Command + V to paste. This method allows seamless integration of linear regions into the grid.

17. How to copy a scene to the Tracks Area in Logic?

- To copy a scene:

  - ◦ Select the Scene trigger button in the grid.
  - ◦ Drag it to the desired position in the Tracks Area. All active cells within the scene will be converted into corresponding regions on the timeline.

18. How to create an Apple Loop from a cell?

- To create an Apple Loop:

  - ◦ Right-click on the cell and choose Export Cell to Apple Loops.
  - ◦ Set the desired loop type (audio or MIDI) and save it to the Apple Loops Library for future use across projects.

19. How can we record audio/MIDI directly into cells in Logic?

- To record directly into a cell:

    ◦ Arm an audio or MIDI track.
    ◦ Click the Record Enable button within the cell.
    ◦ Press Record on the Control Bar or the cell itself to start recording.

- The recorded content will automatically be stored within the selected cell.

20. How can we rename/copy/delete/preview/move/mute/swap cells in Logic Pro?

- Rename: Right-click on a cell > Rename.
- Copy/Delete: Select the cell and press Command + C to copy or Delete to remove.
- Preview: Click on the cell to play it.
- Move: Drag the cell to a new position in the grid.
- Mute: Right-click > Mute.
- Swap: Drag one cell over another while holding Option to swap their content.

21. How can we change loop settings for cells in Live Loops Grid?

- To change loop settings:

    ◦ Select the desired cell and open the Cell Inspector.
    ◦ Adjust the Loop checkbox to enable or disable looping.
    ◦ Set the Loop Length by specifying the number of bars or beats.
    ◦ You can also define the Start and End points to loop a specific section of the cell content.

22. How can we set a cell to ignore Project Tempo in Logic?

- To ignore the project tempo:

    ◦ Select the cell and open the Cell Inspector.

○ In the Tempo section, enable the Ignore Project Tempo checkbox. This allows the cell to play at its original recorded tempo, regardless of the project's overall tempo settings.

23. How can we reverse cell playback in Logic?

- To reverse playback:

  ○ Right-click on the cell and choose Reverse Playback.
  ○ Alternatively, open the Cell Inspector and enable the Reverse option. This flips the audio or MIDI content to play backward, often used for creating unique sound textures.

24. How to focus scenes in Logic?

- To focus on a scene:

  ○ Click on the Scene trigger button to highlight and activate it.
  ○ Use Command + Left/Right Arrow to navigate between scenes.
  ○ Focusing a scene ensures that all its corresponding cells are highlighted, ready for triggering or editing.

25. How can we reorder scenes in Logic?

- To reorder scenes:

  ○ Click and drag the Scene trigger button vertically to a new position in the grid.
  ○ All cells within the scene will move accordingly, updating the playback order during live performances.

26. How can we add an empty scene?

- To add an empty scene:

  ○ Right-click in the Live Loops Grid sidebar and choose Add Empty Scene.
  ○ A blank column will appear, ready to hold new cells or loops.

27. How can we duplicate a scene?

- To duplicate a scene:

    - Right-click on the Scene trigger button and choose Duplicate Scene.
    - All cells within the scene will be copied to a new column with identical settings.

28. How can we delete scenes in Logic?

- To delete a scene:

    - Right-click on the Scene trigger button and select Delete Scene.
    - All cells within that scene will also be removed from the grid.

29. What is the cell editor?

- The Cell Editor is a dedicated interface for editing the content of individual cells:

    - For audio cells, it offers tools for trimming, fading, pitch shifting, and applying effects.
    - For MIDI cells, it provides the Piano Roll for editing notes, velocities, and quantization.
    - Access it by double-clicking any cell or selecting a cell and pressing E.

30. How can we add automation to Live Loops in Logic?

- To add automation:

    - Select the cell and open the Cell Inspector.
    - Click the Automation button.
    - Draw automation curves for parameters like volume, pan, and effects using the Pencil tool.
    - Automations will trigger each time the cell plays, adding dynamic changes to the looped content.

31. How to bounce cells in Logic Pro?

- To bounce cells in Logic Pro, follow these steps:

  - Select the Cell(s): Click on the specific cell or multiple cells in the Live Loops Grid that you want to bounce.
  - Right-click or Use the Menu:

    - Right-click on the selected cell(s) and choose Bounce and Replace Cell from the context menu.
    - Alternatively, go to File > Bounce > Bounce Cells in Place from the top menu bar.

  - Adjust Bounce Settings:

    - A dialog box will appear with options like:

      - Include Effects: Bounce the cell with applied effects.
      - Normalize: Adjust the audio level if needed.
      - Audio Format: Choose between PCM, MP3, or other audio formats.

  - Bounce the Cell:

    - Click OK to complete the process.
    - Logic Pro will render the selected cell as a new audio file, replacing the original cell if selected, or creating a new one alongside it.

- This method is useful when you want to free up CPU resources by bouncing MIDI or complex audio cells into a simpler audio format or to consolidate your work.

TWENTY-TWO
STEP SEQUENCER IN LOGIC PRO

1. What is a step sequencer and how do we use it in Logic Pro?

- A step sequencer is a tool in Logic Pro that allows users to create rhythmic and melodic patterns by assigning notes, velocities, and other parameters to steps on a grid. Each step represents a specific time division, and the sequence loops continuously during playback.
- Usage in Logic Pro:

  - Open the Step Sequencer from the Editors pane or create a new Pattern Region.
  - Each row corresponds to a musical parameter (such as pitch, velocity, or modulation), while columns represent time steps.
  - By clicking on the grid cells, you can activate or deactivate notes, adjust their velocity, and modify other MIDI parameters.
  - The Step Sequencer is especially useful for programming drum beats, basslines, arpeggios, and automation.

2. What are steps and what role does it serve?

- Steps are individual time divisions within the Step Sequencer grid. Each step corresponds to a specific point in time within the pattern.
- Role:

  - Steps are where you input MIDI notes or parameter changes.

- Each step can trigger a note, adjust pitch, modify velocity, or control automation parameters.
- By combining multiple steps, users can create complex rhythmic and melodic patterns.

3. What are patterns and how do we use them in Logic Pro?

- Patterns in Logic Pro are sequences of steps arranged within the Step Sequencer that can be looped and edited.
- Usage:

  - Patterns are created by activating steps in the grid.
  - You can use patterns to build drum loops, basslines, or harmonic sequences.
  - Logic Pro allows saving patterns as templates for reuse, and you can modify them in real-time during playback.

4. How can we create step sequencer patterns in Logic Pro?

- To create step sequencer patterns:

  - Open Logic Pro and create a new project.
  - Add a Software Instrument Track.
  - Right-click on the track region and select Create Pattern Region.
  - Open the Step Sequencer from the editor view.
  - Activate steps on the grid by clicking on them.
  - Adjust parameters like velocity, pitch, and gate for each step.
  - Play the sequence to hear your pattern and make adjustments.

5. How can we create an empty patterns region in Logic?

- To create an empty pattern region:

  - Select the desired track.
  - Go to the top menu and choose Region > Create Pattern Region.
  - An empty grid will appear in the Step Sequencer.
  - You can now manually input steps and configure parameters from scratch.

6. What are step sequencer rows and how are they used in Logic?

- Rows in the Step Sequencer represent different parameters or instruments (such as individual drum hits in a kit, different pitches for a melody, or automation lanes).

  - Usage:

    - Each row is assigned to a specific MIDI note, instrument, or parameter.
    - You can control pitch, modulation, velocity, and even plugin automation from different rows.
    - Rows help organize complex sequences by separating different sound elements.

7. How to enter steps monophonically?

- To enter steps monophonically (one note at a time):

  - Activate the Step Sequencer.
  - Select the Monophonic mode from the settings.
  - Each step entered will replace the previous one within the same row, ensuring that only one note plays at any given time.

8. How to change pattern length in Logic?

- To change pattern length:

  - Open the Step Sequencer.
  - Adjust the Pattern Length slider at the top of the grid.
  - You can set lengths from 1 step to 64 steps or more, depending on your project needs.

9. What is Step Rate and how can we change it in Logic?

- Step Rate determines the speed at which each step is played relative to the project tempo.

- ○ Changing Step Rate:

    - ▪ In the Step Sequencer interface, locate the Step Rate dropdown.
    - ▪ Choose from values such as 1/4, 1/8, 1/16, 1/32 (representing quarter notes, eighth notes, etc.).
    - ▪ Adjusting the step rate changes the rhythm and density of the sequence.

10. What is the role of the Edit Mode selector in the Step Sequencer?

- The Edit Mode selector in Logic Pro's Step Sequencer allows you to switch between editing different parameters for each step.
- Role:

    - ○ Enables toggling between Note mode, Velocity mode, Gate mode, Tie mode, and more.
    - ○ Helps fine-tune each step by allowing changes in pitch, volume, note length, and articulation without leaving the sequencer interface.

11. What types of Rows can we add in the step sequencer?

- In the Step Sequencer of Logic Pro, you can add various types of rows:

    - ○ Note Rows: Assign MIDI notes to specific instruments or pitches.
    - ○ Automation Rows: Automate parameters like filter cutoff, reverb levels, or volume.
    - ○ Velocity Rows: Control the intensity or loudness of each step.
    - ○ Gate Rows: Adjust the length of each triggered note.
    - ○ Tie Rows: Connect consecutive steps for sustained notes.
    - ○ Pitch Rows: Modify the pitch of each step independently.
    - ○ Control Change Rows: Automate MIDI CC parameters like modulation, pan, or expression.

- These rows allow comprehensive sequencing, from note playback to parameter modulation, all within a single interface.

12. What are the Edit modes for Note Rows? Explain them.

- Edit Modes for Note Rows in Logic Pro's Step Sequencer include:

  - Pitch Mode: Adjust the note's pitch for each step.
  - Velocity Mode: Set the velocity of each note, controlling the note's volume or intensity.
  - Gate Mode: Change the duration of each note.
  - Tie Mode: Connect adjacent notes to create longer, sustained sounds.
  - Mute Mode: Silence individual steps without deleting them.
  - Skip Mode: Skips specific steps during playback, adding variation to the pattern.
  - Loop Start/End Mode: Set where the loop starts and ends within a pattern.

- These modes allow precise control over each note's behavior, contributing to more dynamic and complex sequences.

13. What are the different Edit Modes for Automation Rows?

- Automation Rows offer several Edit Modes:

  - Parameter Mode: Select and assign any automation parameter (such as volume, pan, or plugin settings) to the row.
  - Value Mode: Adjust the automation value for each step.
  - Slope Mode: Create smooth transitions between automation values.
  - Cycle Mode: Repeat a set automation pattern across the loop.
  - Random Mode: Generate random values for each step, ideal for adding variation.
  - Step Mode: Assign discrete values to each step manually.

- These modes ensure detailed and dynamic control of automation parameters throughout the sequence.

14. What are subrows and how are they used in Logic?

- Subrows are additional lanes beneath a main row in the Step Sequencer that allow multiple parameters to be controlled simultaneously for the same sequence.
- Usage:

- Each subrow can control a different aspect of the main row (e.g., velocity, pitch, modulation).
- Subrows enable intricate adjustments without needing separate rows for each parameter.
- For example, one row might control note pitch, while its subrows handle velocity, modulation depth, and pan simultaneously.

- This layered control facilitates more nuanced and expressive sequencing.

15. How to show/hide subrows for rows?

- To show/hide subrows in Logic Pro's Step Sequencer:

  - Select a Row in the Step Sequencer.
  - Click the small arrow icon next to the row name to expand or collapse subrows.
  - To add a new subrow, click the "+" button that appears when hovering over the row.
  - You can remove subrows by clicking the "x" on the right side of the subrow lane.

- This feature helps maintain a clean interface while allowing access to detailed controls when needed.

16. How to create ramped values using steps?

- To create ramped values (smoothly changing values across steps):

  - Select the desired Automation Row.
  - Highlight the steps you want to ramp.
  - Right-click and choose Create Ramp.
  - Drag the values manually from low to high (or vice versa), or use the Line Tool to draw a straight ramp across the steps.
  - This creates a gradual increase or decrease, useful for sweeps, crescendos, or parameter automation like filter cutoff modulation.

17. How can we add/remove subrows in Logic?

- To add subrows:

    ◦ Click the "+" button next to the main row in the Step Sequencer.
    ◦ Choose the parameter you wish to control in the subrow (e.g., velocity, modulation).

- To remove subrows:

    ◦ Hover over the subrow you want to delete.
    ◦ Click the "x" that appears on the right side of the subrow.

- This flexibility allows dynamic control and a streamlined workflow.

18. Create a Drum Pattern using the Step Sequencer.

- To create a Drum Pattern:

    ◦ Add a new Software Instrument track and select a Drum Kit.
    ◦ Create a Pattern Region by right-clicking on the track.
    ◦ Open the Step Sequencer Editor.
    ◦ Assign each row to a different drum sound (kick, snare, hi-hat, etc.).
    ◦ Click on steps to activate drum hits for each sound.
    ◦ Adjust velocity subrows for dynamics, add tie steps for sustained sounds, and use automation rows for effects like reverb or panning.

- This results in a fully customizable drum loop.

19. Create a melody using the step sequencer?

- To create a Melody:

    ◦ Add a Software Instrument track with a melodic instrument (e.g., synthesizer, piano).
    ◦ Open the Step Sequencer and select Pitch Rows.
    ◦ Activate steps in a sequence that corresponds to your desired melody.
    ◦ Adjust the pitch for each step using the Pitch Mode.
    ◦ Use velocity rows for dynamic variation and automation rows for effects like vibrato or filter sweeps.

- This method provides precise control over every note in your melody.

20. How to add automations to the step sequencer?

- To add Automations:

  - In the Step Sequencer, click Add Row.
  - Select Automation from the list.
  - Choose the parameter you want to automate (e.g., volume, cutoff frequency).
  - Click on steps to assign automation values.
  - Adjust the values for each step by dragging vertically.
  - Use ramp tools for smooth automation transitions or randomization tools for dynamic variations.

21. What is step recording and how do we do it in the step sequencer in Logic Pro?

- Step Recording allows you to input notes sequentially without real-time performance:

  - Open the Step Sequencer and enable Step Input mode.
  - Select your instrument track and click on the desired starting step.
  - Play notes on a MIDI keyboard or use the Piano Roll to input them.
  - Each note you play is placed on consecutive steps automatically.
  - Adjust pitch, velocity, and gate length for each step to refine the sequence.
  - This method is ideal for precise input of melodies, basslines, and drum patterns.

22. How can we load/save patterns in the Step Sequencer?

- To load patterns:

  - Open the Step Sequencer and click on the Pattern Browser icon.
  - Browse through available preset patterns in Logic's library.
  - Drag and drop a pattern into your sequencer.

- To save patterns:

  - Once your pattern is created, click the File menu > Export > Save Pattern as Preset.
  - Name the pattern and select the location within your Logic Library.
  - Saved patterns can be quickly loaded into future projects, maintaining workflow efficiency.

23. How can we convert a MIDI region to a pattern region?

- To convert:

  - Right-click on any MIDI region in your project.
  - Select Convert to Step Sequencer Pattern Region.
  - The notes from the MIDI region are mapped onto the Step Sequencer grid.
  - This allows you to use step-based editing tools on pre-recorded MIDI, such as adjusting steps, velocities, or automation directly within the Step Sequencer.

24. How can we convert a pattern region to a MIDI region in Logic?

- To convert:

  - Right-click on the Step Sequencer pattern region.
  - Choose Convert to MIDI Region.
  - All sequenced steps are transferred to a traditional MIDI region in the Piano Roll.
  - This is useful when you need detailed MIDI editing beyond the capabilities of the Step Sequencer.

25. How to mute/solo/rotate a row in Logic?

- Mute a Row: Click the M button beside the row.
- Solo a Row: Click the S button to hear only that row.
- Rotate a Row:

  - Select the row.

- ◦ Use the Rotate Left/Right commands in the row settings.
- ◦ Rotation shifts the step sequence, creating rhythmic or melodic variations by changing the step order.

26. How can we change the playback mode of a pattern in the step sequencer?

- Playback modes include:

  - ◦ Forward: Plays steps from left to right.
  - ◦ Reverse: Plays steps from right to left.
  - ◦ Ping-Pong: Plays forward then reverses direction.
  - ◦ Random: Plays steps in random order.
  - ◦ Change playback mode by clicking the Playback Mode menu in the Step Sequencer toolbar and selecting the desired mode.

27. How can we delete unused rows from the step sequencer?

- To delete:

  - ◦ Select the row you wish to remove.
  - ◦ Press Delete or Right-click > Delete Row.
  - ◦ Alternatively, click the row settings icon and choose Remove Row.
  - ◦ This helps keep your sequencer organized by removing unnecessary rows.

28. What is the role of the step sequencer inspector in Logic? Explain the functions the inspector offers.

- The Step Sequencer Inspector provides:

  - ◦ Row Settings: Adjust pitch, velocity, gate length, and more for individual rows.
  - ◦ Global Controls: Set playback speed, direction, and length of the entire pattern.
  - ◦ Automation Management: Control all automation parameters from a single panel.
  - ◦ Pattern Browser: Load and save patterns efficiently.

- ◦ The Inspector acts as the control hub for all sequencing parameters, enhancing precision and creativity.

29. How can we change row colours in Logic?

- To change:

  - ◦ Right-click on the row header.
  - ◦ Select Row Color > Choose Color from the palette.
  - ◦ Assigning colors helps visually distinguish between different rows, especially in complex patterns.

30. What are the ways in which we can customize the Step Sequencer in Logic Pro?

- Customization includes:

  - ◦ Adding/Removing Rows: Tailor the sequencer to your needs.
  - ◦ Changing Grid Resolution: Adjust step lengths for different time divisions (1/16, 1/8, etc.).
  - ◦ Customizing Row Types: Include notes, automation, velocity, and more.
  - ◦ Applying Swing and Groove: Add human-like variations to rigid step patterns.
  - ◦ Saving Templates: Create and save your custom setups for reuse.
  - ◦ Color Coding: Assign specific colors to rows for better visual organization.
  - ◦ Mapping MIDI Controls: Assign hardware controls to Step Sequencer parameters for real-time manipulation.

TWENTY-THREE
QUICK SAMPLER

1. What purpose does the Quick Sampler serve in Logic?

- The Quick Sampler in Logic Pro is a streamlined sampling instrument designed for quickly importing, slicing, and manipulating audio. It serves the purpose of transforming audio recordings into playable instruments by mapping samples across the keyboard. It is particularly useful for:

  - Creating instruments from short audio clips.
  - Slicing loops into individual sections that can be triggered separately.
  - Applying pitch, modulation, and envelope controls to sampled audio.
  - Live performance and quick edits, thanks to its intuitive interface and integration with Logic's MIDI environment.

2. What are the ways in which we can add audio in the Quick Sampler?

- Audio can be added to the Quick Sampler in several ways:

  - Drag and Drop: Simply drag an audio file from the Finder, Logic's Browser, or the Tracks area directly into the Quick Sampler.
  - Record Live: Record audio directly into the sampler by enabling the Record mode and capturing input from a microphone or audio interface.
  - Load from Library: Use the File Browser within Quick Sampler to select and load an existing audio file from Logic's sound library or your system storage.

- ○ Import from Track: Right-click on any audio region in the Tracks area and select Convert to Sampler Track > Quick Sampler.

3. How can we save a Quick Sampler Instrument?

- To save a Quick Sampler instrument:

  - ○ After creating your instrument, click the Save icon in the Quick Sampler interface.
  - ○ Choose Save Instrument As... and provide a name.
  - ○ Logic stores the instrument along with its sample data in the Sampler Instruments folder, making it accessible for future projects.
  - ○ You can also export the instrument using File > Export > All Track as Audio Files, ensuring that your sampler instrument is saved with all project data.

4. What is the Classic Mode in Quick Sampler and what are its uses?

- Classic Mode in Quick Sampler is designed for continuous playback of a sample when a note is held down. Its uses include:

  - ○ Looped playback: Ideal for sustained instruments like strings, pads, or atmospheric textures.
  - ○ Envelope control: Allows detailed manipulation of attack, decay, sustain, and release (ADSR) for shaping the sound.
  - ○ Pitch Modulation: Enables real-time pitch changes based on the MIDI note played.
  - ○ Time-stretching: Keeps the sample in time with the project's tempo while maintaining pitch. This mode is versatile for creating dynamic, evolving sounds from short samples.

5. What is the One Shot mode in Quick Sampler and what are its uses?

- One Shot Mode is optimized for playing the entire sample from start to finish with a single key press, regardless of how long the note is held. Its uses include:

- Drum hits and percussion: Triggering one-shot samples like kicks, snares, or hi-hats.
- Sound effects: Playing sound effects that need to be triggered without looping.
- Vocal chops and stabs: Ideal for triggering short vocal samples or synth stabs in electronic music.
- Fast workflow: Eliminates the need for envelope adjustments as the full sample plays automatically, making it perfect for quickly adding rhythmic or percussive elements.

6. What is the Slice mode in Quick Sampler and what are its uses?

- Slice Mode automatically detects transients in an audio sample and slices it into individual segments, each mapped to a different MIDI key. Its uses include:

  - Chopping loops: Break down drum loops, melodic phrases, or vocal lines into smaller segments.
  - Triggering slices live: Each slice can be played individually, making it useful for live performance and improvisation.
  - Adjusting slice timing and pitch: Each slice can have its own pitch, start point, and envelope settings, providing detailed control over the sample.
  - Rearranging loops: Create entirely new rhythms and sequences by rearranging the slices in the Step Sequencer or Piano Roll.

7. How can we record audio into the Quick Sampler?

- To record audio directly into the Quick Sampler:

  - Open the Quick Sampler in your Logic Pro session.
  - Click on the Record button in the Quick Sampler interface.
  - Select your audio input source from the dropdown menu.
  - Arm the track and hit the Record button within Quick Sampler. This will capture the live audio signal and load it directly into the sampler for further manipulation.
  - Once recorded, the sample is automatically placed in the waveform display, ready for editing and triggering.

8. What are the Start and End markers used for in Logic?

- Start and End markers in Logic are used to define the portion of an audio sample that will be played back within the sampler or timeline. They help in:

  - Trimming the sample to focus on a specific section.
  - Looping a defined region by setting precise loop points.
  - Controlling playback duration without altering the original file. These markers ensure that only the desired part of a sample is used during playback, enhancing accuracy and creative control.

9. What is the use of the Loop Start and Loop End markers?

- Loop Start and End markers determine the section of a sample that will repeat continuously when the sample is played. Their primary uses include:

  - Creating seamless loops for sustained sounds like pads or textures.
  - Controlling loop length and position within the sample.
  - Adjusting loop boundaries dynamically to refine the looping section without affecting the overall sample.

10. What is the function of the crossfade marker?

- The crossfade marker is used to create smooth transitions between the start and end points of a looped sample. It helps:

  - Eliminate clicks or pops that occur when the loop cycles back to the start.
  - Blend the loop seamlessly by gradually fading out the end while fading in the start.
  - Adjust the crossfade duration to suit the sample's characteristics, ensuring a natural, continuous sound loop.

11. What is the Fade In and Fade Out markers used for in Logic?

- Fade In and Fade Out markers control the gradual increase (fade-in) and decrease (fade-out) of a sample's volume. They are essential for:

  - Smoothing the start and end of a sample, preventing abrupt audio entries or cuts.
  - Creating dynamic audio transitions, especially in complex arrangements.
  - Adjusting the fade duration to match the sample's context within a project.

12. How do we use Slice markers in Logic Pro?

- Slice markers are used to divide an audio sample into multiple segments or slices, which can then be triggered independently. In Logic Pro:

  - Open the Quick Sampler and select Slice mode.
  - Logic automatically detects transients and places slice markers at each transient point.
  - You can manually add, delete, or adjust these markers for precise slicing.
  - Each slice can be mapped to individual MIDI notes, allowing for creative rearrangement and triggering.

13. How can we use flex inside the Quick Sampler?

- Flex mode in Quick Sampler enables time-stretching and pitch-shifting without affecting the sample's quality. To use flex:

  - Activate the Flex button in the Quick Sampler.
  - Adjust the Time Stretching algorithm based on the type of sample (e.g., rhythmic, monophonic, polyphonic).
  - Modify the sample's length and tempo independently of pitch, or adjust pitch while maintaining the original tempo. This feature is particularly useful for aligning samples with the project tempo or creating pitch modulation effects.

14. How can we manipulate the ADSR of our Quick Sampler Instrument?

- To manipulate the ADSR envelope in Quick Sampler:

    ◦ Go to the Envelope section in the Quick Sampler interface.
    ◦ Adjust the Attack for how quickly the sound reaches its peak.
    ◦ Modify the Decay to control how long it takes to settle to the sustain level.
    ◦ Set the Sustain level to determine the volume during the held note.
    ◦ Adjust the Release for how long the sound fades out after the note is released. This allows for precise control over the sample's dynamic contour and responsiveness.

15. How can we add a pitch envelope to our Quick Sampler Instrument?

- To add a pitch envelope:

    ◦ Go to the Modulation section of the Quick Sampler.
    ◦ Select Pitch as the destination for the envelope.
    ◦ Adjust the Envelope parameters (ADSR) to determine how pitch changes over time.
    ◦ Set the Amount of pitch modulation to control the range of pitch change. This creates pitch bends and dynamic shifts within the sample's playback.

16. What are the different Snap Modes in the Quick Sampler? Explain them.

- Snap Modes control how audio edits snap to grid points in Logic Pro:

    ◦ Off: No snapping, allowing free movement.
    ◦ Smart: Snaps based on the current zoom level, providing flexibility.
    ◦ Bar/Beat/Division/Tick: Snaps to specific musical time units, such as bars, beats, or subdivisions. These modes ensure precise sample editing, especially for rhythmic elements.

17. What are the different Loop Modes in the Quick Sampler and how do they behave?

- Loop Modes in Quick Sampler include:

- ◦ No Loop: Plays the sample once.
- ◦ Forward Loop: Repeats the sample from start to end continuously.
- ◦ Reverse Loop: Loops the sample in reverse.
- ◦ Ping-Pong Loop: Alternates between forward and reverse playback for each loop cycle. Each mode offers unique playback characteristics suitable for different sound design needs.

18. How can we glide between notes when using the Quick Sampler?

- To enable glide (portamento):

  - ◦ Go to the Pitch section in the Quick Sampler.
  - ◦ Activate the Glide control.
  - ◦ Adjust the glide time to set how quickly the pitch transitions between notes. This creates smooth pitch slides between consecutive notes, ideal for leads, basslines, and experimental textures.

The Journey Ahead In Music Production

As we reach the conclusion of this guide, it is important to recognize that music production is a continuous journey of learning, experimentation, and creative evolution. Mastering tools like Logic Pro and Ableton Live is not just about understanding their functions—it is about developing a workflow that enhances your artistic vision.

This book has provided a structured approach to answering common questions, helping you navigate technical challenges and refine your production skills. However, true expertise comes with practice, curiosity, and a willingness to explore beyond the given answers.

As you continue your journey, embrace the ever-changing landscape of music technology, stay updated with new techniques, and never stop experimenting with sound. Let this guide be a foundation, not a limit—your creativity and innovation will always be the most powerful tools in music production.

Thank you for allowing this book to be part of your learning process. May your passion for music and your dedication to mastering your craft lead you to create extraordinary sounds that resonate with the world.

Aritra Sarkar